A Theology of

A Theology of
FORCE AND VIOLENCE

Peter Mayhew

SCM PRESS
London

TRINITY PRESS INTERNATIONAL
Philadelphia

First published 1989

SCM Press
26–30 Tottenham Road
London N1 4BZ

Trinity Press International
3725 Chestnut Street
Philadelphia, Pa. 19104

*Unless otherwise stated, biblical quotations are taken
from the New English Bible*

British Library Cataloguing in Publication Data
Mayhew, Peter
  A theology of force and violence.
  1. Violence. Moral and religious aspects
  I. Title
  261.8'3

  ISBN 0–334–02360–2

Library of Congress Cataloging-in-Publication Data
Mayhew, Peter.
    A theology of force and violence / Peter Mayhew.
      p.   cm.
    ISBN 0–334–02360–2
    1. Violence—Religious aspects—Christianity.   I. Title.
      BT736.15.M34   1989   89–4491
      241'.697—dc20

Photoset by J & L Composition Ltd, Filey, North Yorks
and printed in Great Britain by
Richard Clay Ltd, Bungay, Suffolk

This book is dedicated to
the Right Reverend Lloyd Morrell,
formerly Bishop of Lewes

Contents

	Preface	ix
1	Force and the Gospel	1
2	Justice	8
3	Three Men of Peace	16
4	Violence in Northern Ireland	34
5	Palestine, South Africa, Central and South America	53
6	War	89
7	What Now?	100
	Notes	103
	Index	109

Preface

I have written this short book because of the ever-growing significance to me of the Christian doctrine of justice. This doctrine seems to me to need to be defended and propagated at the present time. I reckon that a belief in the need of force to promote justice was conceived in me soon after my conversion to the Christian faith. This had come about gradually in the early 1930s under the influence of a wonderful friend only a few years older than myself. At first my new-found faith inclined me to pacifism and to agreement with a famous resolution passed at a debate in the Oxford Union Society on 8 February 1933: 'This House would not fight for King and country.' However, the obvious evil of Nazi rule in Germany which had begun earlier that year opened my eyes to the well-meaning wrong-headedness of the pacifist movement. The sufferings which Hitler inflicted on others in his country and with which he threatened the peoples of other countries could not be tolerated by Christians indefinitely. The Germans had lost all their freedom; imprisonment, torture and killings were rampant. There was no secret about all this. The newspapers were full of the details, and excerpts from them are before me on this table. I myself instructed the pupils at the Blackburn Grammar School, the school in the north of England where I was teaching, out of the pages of the *Brown Book of the Hitler Terror*. I read now from an excerpt from an English newspaper of the events of 8 November 1938, 'Kristallnacht' (the 'Night of the Broken Glass'):

The whole of Germany's Jewish community was tonight subjected to a reign of terror without precedent in modern times in a civilized country . . . In Berlin fashionably dressed women clapped and screamed with laughter and some held up their babies to watch the Jews being beaten senseless by youths with lead piping.

I had learned liberal politics under Professor Harold Laski, and I had sat under Professor R. H. Tawney. However, it was my new-found religion which drove me into the realization that the Germans and all Europe must be rescued forcibly from all this, if it was not already too late for such a rescue. I went over to Germany, stayed in Frankfurt and Munich and in Cologne (after the German re-occupation of the Rhineland); I tried to see and hear all I could of what was going on, learning from the whispers of decent, kindly German people who all ceased to be as Nazi rule went on.

I did not at that time think at all in terms of justice and injustice; I had not yet heard of, let alone absorbed, the Christian doctrine of justice. My interest in it developed during my post-War years in Australia. Towards the end of my time there as Headmaster of a South Queensland Bush Brotherhood boarding school, three different boys at different times chose with exquisite politeness to refuse my punishment. The ground for their refusal in every case was that I was being, in their opinion, unjust. These incidents caused me to think furiously concerning justice and its meaning. There came from my unconscious into my conscious mind the words 'Fiat justitia, ruat coelum' ('Let justice be done though the skies fall'). Some years later in a mining town in North-West Queensland, I was involved in a devastating industrial dispute in which the miners of Mount Isa accused the excellent but undiscerning management of injustice towards them. I failed lamentably in my passionate attempts to explain one side to the other. In my frustration I vowed then and there that, if ever I had the chance, I would devote hard study to the significance of the concept of justice. Some years later, in the 1970s and 1980s, I found myself back in Oxford and able to do just that.

In the New English Bible translation, St Matthew's Gospel tells us that Jesus said: 'Set your mind on God's kingdom and his justice before everything else' (6.33). In St Paul's Epistle to the Romans I read: 'The kingdom of God is not eating and drinking, but justice . . .' (14.17). My New Testament scholar friend tells me that 'justice' is really not a good translation in these places. I am unconcerned. I believe in the whole biblical and philosophical doctrine of justice, one not dependent on a verse here and a verse there. I continue to glory, however, in the words of the prophet Amos: 'Let justice roll on like a river' (5.24). Injustice affects lives; if justice is attacked, it may be necessary to take lives and to lose lives in order to save lives.

I ought to add that I am not a militant type. I always disliked fighting as a child, probably because of sheer cowardice. I did not enjoy my war experience of battle. On the other hand, I never felt easy about being a spectator, least of all of other people's sufferings. As a spectator of suffering, I had a sense of guilt unless I was trying to do something about it. I believe that we must concern ourselves with the righting of wrong. We are our brothers' keepers and must face up to our responsibilities. It is mere sentimentality to imagine that we are trying to love our neighbours if we are not concerned about injustice towards them. When my vicar gave thanks to God in church at the beginning of October 1938 for the peace worked out at Munich between Neville Chamberlain, M. Daladier, Hitler and Mussolini, at the cost of the freedom of Czecho-Slovakia, I shouted loudly within myself, 'No, no, no!' In three days' time Hitler would be marching into the Sudetenland. I was frightened but intensely relieved when war came on 3 September 1939.

All that I have written has been read by two esteemed friends more learned than myself. I have tried to incorporate into my text the suggestions they have made for its improvement. I am grateful to my friend, the Revd Bob Morgan, for the help which he has given me (without agreeing with me) concerning my New Testament references, and to Dr Peter Hinchliff for checking my writing about South Africa. Edwin Robertson has been good enough to read and correct all I have written about Dietrich Bonhoeffer. Canon Bill Daley of Belfast Cathedral has helped me personally about Northern Ireland, and has read all I have written about it (without endorsing it all). Professor David Apter of Yale, when in Oxford in 1988, gave me most graciously of his time as well as an account of his personal and intimate experience of terrorists in different parts of the world. The Revd Christopher Bryant is responsible for arousing my interest in and concern for Latin America. Sister Pamela Hussey SHC, of the Catholic Institute for International Relations, and Dr Peter West, of Church Action for Central America, have been marvellously helpful to me concerning Latin America and liberation theology. My friend Daniel Burton, freshly back in mid-1988 from two years' experience of life in the Occupied Territories of Palestine, has supplied me with invaluable information. Sister Margaret of the Society of All Saints has been kind enough once more with great efficiency to type out all I have written. The book is dedicated to the friend who taught me the Christian faith.

CHAPTER ONE

Force and the Gospel

When I mentioned to a small group of Christians that I proposed to write a *Theology of Force and Violence*, a young Oxford College Chaplain remarked that I would 'have trouble with the New Testament'. He was no doubt thinking of the teaching of the Sermon on the Mount. I do not believe that he was right.

According to St Matthew's Gospel, Jesus seems to have declared that there is to be for the Christian no self-defence and no retaliation. 'If someone slaps you on the right cheek, turn and offer him your left' (5.39). According to the Revised Standard Version, he is not to 'resist one who is evil' (5.44). According to St Luke's Gospel, there is to be no protection for private property, it appears. 'When a man takes your coat, let him have your shirt as well' (6.29). Again according to St Luke, the Christian must never seemingly turn his back on the borrower. He must 'lend without expecting any return' (6.35). If all this had been intended to be taken literally and to be of universal application, it would have been an invitation to anarchy.

I heard an excellent and sincere pacifist priest recently declare that these precepts are 'the essence of the ethical teaching of Jesus'. The priest was applauded by many. I do not believe that they are the essence of the ethical teaching of Jesus. The ethical teaching of Jesus, according to the New Testament, includes his endorsement of the Mosaic Law and of the prophets. 'Do not suppose that I have come to abolish the Law and the prophets,' he said. 'So long as heaven and earth endure, not a letter, not a stroke will disappear from the Law' (Matt. 5.17–18). This, too, is not to be taken literally; but it has significance and ought not to be ignored as if it were not in the New Testament.

Justice is a mighty prophetic principle; Christ demanded that it be rendered in love. 'Set your mind on God's kingdom and his justice before everything else,' he said, according to the Gospel of St Matthew (6.33 NEB). If the precepts from the Sermon on the Mount referred to in the previous paragraphs were invariably to be acted on, justice would be flouted, chaos would set in, and evil would come to reign. They were, however, intended to challenge Christians to think before reacting to wrong-doing in a forceful way. We are rightly warned again and again against using force too readily. There are occasions when non-resistance and the acceptance of undeserved suffering may have a converting influence. Nevertheless, the bully and the robber and the rapist will frequently have to be met by the Christian with force. It would normally be quite wrong for the Christian to stand by while the weak are maltreated and to call his attitude an expression of the ethical teaching of Jesus.

Indeed, writes Professor Dennis Nineham, words counselling non-resistance do not command any validity 'isolated from their original context'. That context is the whole Gospel of Jesus Christ. 'Every theological student', Dr Nineham says, has 'to set a biblical verse or passage in its correct *Sitz-im-Leben* (situation in life) before seeking to interpret or expound it.'

Dr Nineham shows that for Jesus love of God and love of one's neighbour were the laws which underlay all the Mosaic Law, and that 'complete love of God and the neighbour' were the key to the meaning of the lesser precepts which he taught his disciples to keep.[1] The lesser are subordinate to the greater; love of God and love of neighbour are outraged if the Christian stands by and sees his neighbour battered.

The Gospel precepts of Jesus, as we have seen, are not laws for universal application. They are rather provocative challenges to hard thinking and sometimes to hard decision. The Bishop of Oxford rightly says that 'Jesus was not a legalist . . . he did not lay down detailed rules about how we are to behave in any and every situation.'[2] Christ's method of moral teaching was not to issue edicts but to say striking and challenging things, to use hyperbole, exaggeration, parables, to induce people to ask themselves what he really means and what they should really do. Neither retaliation nor the invoking of the law is always the answer to wrong-doing. Force must only be used with care and discretion. Neither is the turning of the other cheek and a policy of non-resistance always the Christian's duty.

Usually the Christian's obligation is to protect the innocent and to prevent further wrong-doing, using force only if necessary. Otherwise thieving, destruction, killing develop in Christian society. There is normally nothing Christian, nothing in tune with the Sermon on the Mount, in facilitating evil by doing nothing.

Karl Rahner, the eminent Jesuit theologian, wrote:

The principle of the absolute renunciation of force would not . . . be a Christian principle. It would be a heresy which misunderstood the nature of man, his sinfulness and his existence as the interplay of persons in the *one* space of material being. An order of freedom would be misunderstood, if it were taken to be an order of things in which

3

force was considered reprehensible on principle. A fundamental and universal renunciation of physical force of all kinds is not merely impracticable. It is also immoral because it would mean the self-destruction of the subject who is responsible to God.[3]

It would also mean the destruction of others for whom we are responsible to God. However, if the use of force is frequently necessary to restrain the wrong-doer, Jesus by his teaching in the Sermon on the Mount is telling us to consider whether on certain occasions the wrong-doer ought not to be allowed to get away with it. Sometimes, not frequently, as I have already suggested, mercy may make the wrong-doer think. St Paul has caught the spirit of his Master's teaching when he writes: 'Never pay back evil for evil. If possible ... live at peace with all men ... Do not seek revenge ... If your enemy is hungry, feed him ... use good to defeat evil' (Rom. 12.17–21). He rightly sees no incongruity with the mind of that same Master, when he immediately goes on to justify 'the power of the sword': 'Every person must submit to the supreme authorities ... You wish to have no fear of the authorities? ... But if you are doing wrong, then you will have cause to fear them; it is not for nothing that they hold the power of the sword ...' (Rom. 13.1–4).

For Christians obliged to use force there is to be no hatred and no spirit of revenge. I think of our troops who protected frightened German prisoners-of-war from angry Belgians on the weary road to Dunkirk in 1940. The prisoners were not released to the Belgians; they were kept safe from them. Japanese prisoners-of-war in Burma were almost overwhelmed by the British troops with cups of hot sweet tea and cigarettes in 1944–5. On the other hand, with no qualms of conscience, I took care this morning to do all I could to prevent my drunken young friend who knocked a girl off her bicycle from pursuing further activities of this kind. The use of force is by no means to be casually invoked by Christians. Sometimes, however, it has to be used promptly and effectively to protect the weak and the innocent.

If non-resistance on all occasions were truly Christ's teaching and the Christian's duty, order would cease to be. 'What are kingdoms without justice but large bands of robbers?'[4] says St Augustine. According to John's Gospel, Jesus said to Pontius Pilate that if his kingdom belonged to this world, then his servants would fight (18.36). Christians are called into the kingdom of God, and the kingdom of God is beginning to be formed in the midst of us. It has to be sought and sacrificed for; it cannot, of course, be gained by force of arms. However, those of us who seek to win and to maintain faithful membership of it still belong to earthly 'kingdoms'. We must be good citizens of those kingdoms; we must be prepared to support and defend the order they embody, at least in so far as we believe that they are not demanding of us what is contrary to the will of God. According to the gospel, Jesus indeed said, 'my servants would fight' (RSV). Jesus in the gospel seems to assume that faithful Christians have sometimes an obligation to fight, not of course for the kingdom of God, but for 'the kingdoms of this world' to which they continue to belong and to which they have obligations, even though they are already in embryo citizens of the kingdom of God. The kingdom of God 'close to you' (Luke 10.9) must not cause us to withdraw from the earthly kingdom, so long as earthly kingdoms are necessary. We must keep laws, unless they seem to us contrary to the will of God; we must pay taxes, we must promote and defend justice. Karl Jaspers wrote:

> There exists among men, because they are men, a solidarity through which each shares responsibility for every injustice and every wrong committed in the world ... If I do not do whatever I can to prevent them, I am an accomplice in

them. If I have not risked my life in order to prevent the murder of other men, if I have stood silent, I feel guilty.[5]

Let me be still more repetitive, in order to make a far from obvious point more strongly and clearly. Modern understanding of the Bible demands that we refuse to take single texts from the Sermon on the Mount or elsewhere in the Bible and treat them as authoritative directives irrespective of the rest of the teaching of Christianity. As we have seen, Jesus' method of teaching was normally to challenge his hearers into hard thinking as to his real meaning, both by parables and by striking sayings not intended to be taken always, if ever, literally. As a result of such hard thinking, he hoped that his hearers would come to decisions as to the right courses for them to take under varying circumstances. All too often for our peace of mind, we are faced with moral dilemmas; non-resistance is by no means the only possible right answer to evil. We shall see in Chapter 3 that Dietrich Bonhoeffer under the Nazi régime was obliged to make the appalling decision between remaining a well-meaning but passive spectator as wickedness and suffering spread about him, and the breaking of two of the Ten Commandments in order to try to bring this wickedness and suffering to an end. Professors Bruce Chilton and J. I. H. McDonald refer to Bultmann's contention that existential decisions should be placed at the centre of a systematic understanding of Jesus' teaching.[6] J. L. Houlden writes that 'it is only in the situation that ... a decision can be made'.[7]

I have tried to show that neither the Bible as a whole, nor the teaching of Jesus in particular, prohibits the use of force. On the other hand, the teaching of Jesus makes it very clear that governments and Christian people are seriously challenged to think hard before they make the existential decision to use it or to support its use. Force may well lead to violence and neither will, of itself, build up the kingdom of God. On the other hand, a failure to use force may lead to cruel repression rather than to the kingdom. The great offence against human and Christian values which may require Christians and others to emply force is injustice.

Paul Tillich told us that 'we have to apply force, otherwise ... we would sacrifice the justice which is the principal form of all social life'.[8] If injustice is to be forcefully opposed, it is important that those who forcefully oppose it should also be engaged in the detailed planning of a society which will ensure justice. As we shall see in Chapter 5, it is the strength of some South and Central American revolutionaries that they do plan for the detailed construction of a just order simultaneously with their planning for the overthrow of an unjust one. I shall try to explain in the next chapter what we mean by justice itself: not merely the rule of law, but the full acknowledgment in theory and practice of human dignity. I have been repetitive in this chapter in an attempt to make sure of driving home an interpretation of New Testament teaching which is traditional but not common these days.

CHAPTER TWO

Justice

The basic theme of this writing is that justice is all-important for human beings and that the establishment of it must be fought for if it cannot be secured by any other means. The attempt to maintain peace by the use of non-violence will not normally secure that justice which is the necessary basis for peace. Peace will not be secure without justice; human nature will not and must not tolerate injustice indefinitely. There will come, in the end, outbreaks of violence; and there will grow, in an uneasy state of peace, an uneasy fear of where and when the next outbreak will be. The violence of oppression as we have seen it in operation in the Gaza Strip and the West Bank and in South Africa on our television screens will inevitably breed the wilder, less co-ordinated violence of the oppressed against their oppressors. The force and violence with which apartheid is administered invites force and violence against the ministers of apartheid. Whenever there seems to be no end in view to a régime of injustice, outbreaks of violence at first to protest against it, in the end to overthrow it, become inevitable. Human nature craves for justice and will not be interminably denied it.

Christians have to be sympathetic with outbreaks of revolutionary violence against prolonged injustice, although they cannot always condone them. The Lambeth Conference of Anglican bishops at Canterbury in 1988 declared itself 'understanding' of the 'armed struggle' in such circumstances (although not in Ireland). Pope Pius XII was a Christian leader whose learning, wisdom and integrity made him respected by many Christians outside his own communion. His encyclical letter *Populorum Progressio* of 1967 has been described as 'one of the most important social documents issued since Vatican II'. In it he warns, in paragraph 31, that 'revolutionary risings' may 'engender new injustices, introduce new inequities'. Revolutionaries have to take care to see that they do not produce 'an even worse result' as a sequel to their activity. However, in paragraphs 29, 30 and 32, the Pope spoke with great energy:

> We must make haste. Too many people are suffering ... The injustice of certain situations cries out for God's attention ... We want to be clearly understood on this point: the present state of affairs must be confronted boldly, and its concomitant injustices must be challenged and overcome.

So he comes to the point, in paragraph 31, where he allows for 'revolutionary uprisings ... where there is manifest, long-standing tyranny which would do great damage to fundamental personal rights and dangerous harm to the common good of the country'. He sanctions under these circumstances the use of revolutionary force. We must have some tolerance for those who are obsessed with his plea for haste and boldness but who lack the capacity for the 'measured steps' to 'maintain the proper equilibrium' which he recommends for less serious cases. He himself seems to understand (paragraph 30):

Lacking the bare necessities of life, whole nations are under the thumb of others; they cannot act on their own initiative; they cannot exercise personal responsibility; they cannot work towards a higher degree of cultural refinement or a greater participation in social and public life. They are sorely tempted to redress these insults to their human nature by violent means.

He rightly counsels restraint in the use of revolutionary force against injustice. He, no doubt, had in mind the wisdom of St Thomas Aquinas who warned against the danger of substituting a new tyranny for an old one, and that of the Spanish theologian Suarez (1548–1617), who counselled 'prudence' lest a 'greater injury to the people' be brought about.[1]

The basic meaning of justice itself is not a matter of law and law courts. Sometimes indeed courts of law may be unjust in their decisions. Edmund Burke described justice as 'the eternal principle of human dignity'. Paul Tillich referred to it as 'the principal form of all social life'.[2] It binds people together as they practise it towards one another. It does indeed mean the recognition of human dignity, the paying of the respect that is due to each human being.

Bruno Snell tells us that the concept of the dignity of man conquered the philosophic thought of Greece. 'Something new was added, and that was sympathy with one's fellow-man.'[3] The great Greek philosophers tried to define it. Plato in *The Republic* declared that the greatest wrong one can do to others is injustice.[4] Aristotle is more positive. Justice is 'the good of others'.[5] One must take from man nothing that is properly his, render to him all that is rightly his. Sir Ernest Barker wrote that 'the same word justice serves Aristotle, as it served Plato, for goodness and law-abidingness, for the virtue of man and the virtue of citizen'.[6]

The ethical teaching of Jesus assumed the ethical teaching of the Old Testament prophets of the eighth century BC. To some extent this powerful prophetic teaching is concealed from modern readers by the Authorized Version of the Bible which tends to mistranslate the Hebrew word for justice. The word *mishpat* is better translated in newer versions. It is righteousness in operation, the justice of God towards his people, the righteousness in practice of his people towards one another. Of course it includes an element of judgmentalism, of the condemnation of unrighteousness on the part of the righteous God and of his would-be holy people. The justice of God demands justice amongst his people, condemns their injustice towards one another. In God's name, the prophet Amos speaks: 'I know ... how countless your sins, you who persecute the guiltless ... thrust the destitute out of court.' He goes on: 'Let justice roll on like a river' (5.12 and 24).

'The Lord', writes the prophet Isaiah, 'is a God of justice' (30.18). 'The Lord is just and loves just dealing,' the psalmist assures us (11.7). God's throne, he goes on to tell us, 'is built upon righteousness and justice' (89.14). Dr N. H. Snaith sums up the prophetic teaching by telling us that for Israel justice was 'closely intertwined with religion'.[7] 'What is it that the Lord asks of you?' queries Micah. 'Only to act justly,' he replies for God (6.8).

Jesus, as we have seen, accepted the teaching of justice by the Old Testament prophets. 'Always treat others as you would like them to treat you: that is the law and the prophets,' he proclaimed (Matt. 7.12). He preached a kingdom of God in which, surely, God's justice would be respected, his will done. St Paul echoed him: 'The kingdom of God is not eating and drinking, but justice' (Rom. 14.17). As we have seen, doubt has been cast as to whether the word 'justice' is a valid translation here. St Thomas Aquinas in the thirteenth century took the Christian doctrine of justice and wedded it to that of Aristotle. 'Justice is a habit', he wrote, 'whereby a man renders to each one his due.'[8] Justice, he tells us, directs people in their dealings with others.[9] 'It is the master-virtue,' he wrote, 'commanding and prescribing what is right.'[10] On all this is founded the church's teaching of the first of the 'cardinal virtues', justice. Dr A. J. Carlyle wrote of mediaeval Christians that, despite their shortcomings, they did firmly believe that justice was the first and last principle of social life.[11]

Modern Christians, with their high-principled and well-intentioned concentration upon the virtue of love, have often neglected in their thinking and speaking the importance of justice as a basis for truly loving relationships, as a sure foundation for the higher virtue. The distinguished Protestant theologian, Emil Brunner, declared that 'justice is always the pre-condition of love', that 'the real gift of love begins where justice has been done', that 'love always presupposes justice'.[12] John Bennett, the former President of Union Theological Seminary, New York, writes that 'love should will justice', that 'love and justice come together'.[13]

Pope Pius XII demanded in the name of justice that 'all recognize and respect the sacred rights of liberty and human dignity'. The millions who hate war, who fear nuclear war, who abominate violence in Northern Ireland and in South Africa and Israel, must face up to the fact of human life that violence in one form or another is likely in the face of that injustice which seems to be unending and immovable. When we come to study revolutionary movements in Northern Ireland we shall see that the so-called terrorists try not to think of the people they are attacking, but only of the causes which those (mostly uniformed) people represent. I myself in India during the late thirties met and made friends with charming young Indians dedicated to the expulsion of the British, if necessary by violence. They neither showed nor felt any animosity towards individual Britishers, but were determined to drive out the régime, at whatever cost.

The Lambeth bishops in the summer of 1988 chose to

'support' 'the way of non-violence as being the way of our Lord, including direct non-violent action, civil disobedience and conscientious objection'. They presumably reconciled this in their minds with their formal claim to 'understand' those who, 'after exhausting all other ways, choose the way of armed struggle as the only way to justice'. They were emphatic that 'there is no true peace without justice, and that the reformation and transformation of unjust systems is an essential element of our biblical hope'. At the urgent request of some of the Irish bishops, they later condemned all violence in Ireland.

Those who seek lasting peace must indeed seek lasting justice within nations and between nations. Injustice tends to continue until it is forcibly attacked. We shall study in Chapter 3 seeming exceptions to this 'rule' in the cases of the non-violent campaigns for justice of Mahatma Gandhi and Martin Luther King. We shall try to see if their non-violent methods might be successful elsewhere. When the Right Hon. Gerald Kaufman MP visited the Gaza Strip in 1988 in the midst of the bitter anti-Israeli violence by the Arab majority in that area, he remarked that 'a satisfactory solution is ultimately inevitable'. There is, however, nothing inevitable about an end to violence so long as injustice persists. *The Guardian* commented:

> Mr Shamir ... may think it is only a matter of time before the rioters run out of steam. He may even for a time be right. But if the root cause is not tackled the riots will resume, each round worse than the last. He has only to look south towards Pretoria for confirmation.[14]

Injustice may well go on and on; but its continuance will be punctuated by violence against it, until at last violence overthrows it. Hitler's Gauleiter of Bavaria, Adolf Wagner, prophesied before the Second World War that the Nazi régime would last a thousand years. As I listened on the radio to an account of this speech, I felt a wild sense of fear that this might be true, given the apparent complete lack of opposition to Hitlerism within Germany. I had not reckoned on a Bonhoeffer; but the Bonhoeffer plot on the Führer's life failed. In fact, it took the mighty forces of the United States, the Soviet Union and the British Empire to bring the incarnate injustice of the Third Reich to an end in 1945.

'Peace', said the Catholic Bishops at Medellín in 1968, 'is a dynamic process through which justice is established.' Rather, it is justice which is a dynamic process through which peace is established. It is justice which Christians and others must persevere to achieve if they want peace. The Bishops spoke more accurately at Medellín when they said that peace is 'a work of justice, an ever renewed task'. We shall see in Chapter 5 how some South American revolutionaries realize that amongst those with whom they are working towards revolution they must simultaneously be working towards the construction of a just society. Sir Samuel Hoare and others before the Second World War thought for a time that there might be a lasting peace between Hitler and Britain and France. Mr Neville Chamberlain, the Prime Minister, returned from Munich in 1938, claiming that he brought with him 'peace in our time'. Neither of these English statesmen seemed to realize that there could be no lasting international peace while gross injustice prevailed in and around Nazi Germany.

The gentle, thoughtful, peace-loving President Kaunda of Zambia has said that violence can only be justified, and then only as a last resort, when it is directed against an order in which violence itself is implicit. Read of the violence with which South Africa retains a semblance of peace in the black townships; watch on television the Israeli troops 'at work' against Palestinian boys. There is violence maintaining injustice. Against such an order violence is sometimes justified and may often be right.

President Kaunda is wise and good, and his defence of violence is restrained. He says of non-violence that it 'can only be fully effective against a morally sensitive opponent'.[15] We shall recall this when we consider Mahatma Gandhi and Martin Luther King and their campaigns of non-violence in the next chapter. Moral sensitivity is uncommon among those who oppress; but it is not unknown.

CHAPTER THREE

Three Men of Peace

The case against force and for non-violence was made by M. K. Gandhi in his speeches and in his writings, and, above all, by his dedicated life. Mahatma ('Great Soul') Gandhi is likely to be remembered as the outstanding twentieth-century protagonist of non-violent action as the best method of righting wrong and of achieving freedom for a people. 'For me,' he wrote, 'non-violence is not a mere philosophical principle. It is the rule and breath of my life.'[1] He believed that India would not be freed from British rule unless the people as a whole were converted to non-violence. Great though his influence was, he did not succeed in converting them. Even close colleagues like the first Prime Minister of a free India, Jawaharlal Nehru, were not converted to it. In 1947 India was indeed liberated, but not by Gandhi's series of non-violent campaigns.

Mohandas Karamchand Gandhi was born in Porbandar in Gujarat, north-west of Bombay, in 1869. He belonged to a basically Hindu sect which incorporated certain Muslim elements. He was married at the age of twelve. In 1888, he went to Britain to read law in London, and was called to the Bar in 1891. In April 1893 he went to Durban to practise law in the British Crown Colony of Natal. Here he began to experience and to appreciate fully the extent of white prejudice against 'coloured' people. His concern was primarily for his Indian fellow-countrymen. He proved himself in South Africa an effective advocate, organizer and leader in the struggle for Indians' rights. Here, before the Boer War, he came to the conclusion that personal dedication was necessary for himself and that non-violence was the means he and others must pursue against British and Dutch intolerance in South Africa. In 1896, he took a vow of chastity,[2] which he called *brahmacharya*. Henceforth, he would abstain from sexual intercourse, as well as from meat and eggs and all animal products. Later, fasting was to become a major spiritual and political element in his life. He took great care of his body, and when he returned to India, caused it to be massaged with mustard oil and lime juice for forty-five minutes each day.[3] He had developed in South Africa, in theory and in practice, a policy of *ahimsa*, of passive resistance against unjust laws. This whole strategy of refusal to obey the unjust, combined with a willingness to suffer the consequences of disobedience, he called *satyagraha* ('truth force').[4] Non-violence would only succeed if practised by the self-disciplined. On his return with his family to India in 1915, he set up a community on the Sabarmati River, near Ahmedabad in the Bombay Presidency. Here his disciples practised *brahmacharya, satyagraha, ahimsa*, worked at spinning and weaving, accepted as their equals a number of 'untouchables', and boycotted imported English cloth.[5]

Gandhi claimed, with sincerity, to love the British. He wrote: 'I ask and desire nothing but the barest justice that is due to us.'[6] He won the respect of the Indian National Congress, and attended its session in 1916. In 1922, his Congress colleagues urged him to lead the country into mass civil disobedience. He served twenty-two months in gaol for inciting civil disobedience. In February 1930, he warned the Viceroy, Lord Irwin, that he proposed to lead a civil disobedience march against the salt laws which safeguarded the government's monopoly of salt-making. This governmental system of imposed monopoly he referred to as 'organized violence'. He wrote: 'If you cannot see your way to deal with these evils . . . on the eleventh day of this month, I shall proceed, with such co-workers of the ashram as I can take, to disregard the provisions of the salt laws.'[7] He proceeded to lead seventy-eight of his followers from the ashram to Dandi on the coast. Theirs was a two hundred and forty-one mile walk, and it took twenty-eight days. The journey attracted world-wide attention. At the end of it the marchers prayed; they then took salt water from the sea and allowed the water to evaporate on the beach. The salt became available for consumption, and this broke the salt laws. V. Mehta writes: 'Up and down the coasts . . . peoples became *satyagrahis* and broke the law . . . By midsummer, according to one estimate, as many as a hundred thousand *satyagrahis*, including most of the major and minor Congress leaders, were in jail.'[8] A smaller number, sixty-one thousand perhaps, seems more likely. Gandhi himself had been arrested on 5 May, but was released from prison in January 1931. He was to have talks with the Viceroy in New Delhi. He had altogether eight sessions with Lord Irwin, including twenty-four hours of discussion.

In 1939, India found herself at war with Germany, because Britain was at war. In 1940, Gandhi initiated a civil disobedience campaign which consisted of a series of individual acts of civil disobedience. In August 1942, after Japan had joined the German side in the Second World War, and after the failure of a Mission led by Sir Stafford Cripps, Gandhi thought it right to encourage the Congress to launch a new and mass civil disobedience campaign under the title of 'Quit

India'. All Congress workers were 'to consider themselves thenceforth free of British rule'.[9] On 9 August, the Congress leaders, including Gandhi, were arrested and imprisoned. Gandhi and his wife and entourage were housed in the Aga Khan's 'palace' at Yeravda on the Ahmednagar road, just outside Poona. Opposite the 'palace', across the road, was the 2nd Battalion the Manchester Regiment, to which I was attached. We had recently arrived from Britain. The 2nd British Division to which we belonged became responsible for Gandhi and his colleagues during the time when it was feared that there might be a serious Japanese invasion of India. On 6 May 1944, after fasting and ill-health, Gandhi was finally released. India was relatively at peace, the European War nearly won; it seemed that it was safe to free him.

British politicians and educated Britishers had been favourable to India's movement towards independence before the great Salt March. As early as 1818, the Governor General, the Marquess of Hastings, had written that at a 'not very remote time' England would 'wish to relinquish the dominion which she has ... assumed'.[10] H. V. Hodson writes: 'From the time of Sir Thomas Munro and Thomas Babington Macaulay there was ... a strand of aspiration to lead the peoples of India to a condition in which they would be able to govern themselves and grow out of imperial tutelage.'[11] As early as 1918, the Montagu-Chelmsford Report declared that 'Indians must be enabled to determine for themselves what they want done ... The process will begin in local affairs ... it will proceed to the complete control of provincial matters, and thence, in the course of time and subject to the proper discharge of Imperial responsibilities, to the control of matters concerning all India.' The development of the self-governing Dominions, with which India in various Imperial Conferences became closely associated, pointed the British people towards similar development for India itself. Those educated persons in Britain who saw Canada, Australia, New Zealand, Newfoundland and the

Union of South Africa obviously capable of self-government saw no reason why India too should not become capable. Only inter-communal tensions seemed to some an almost insoluble problem.

Gandhi's visit to Britain to represent the Congress at the second Round Table Conference in 1931 had made an extraordinary impression in Britain. Thousands of Indian students at British universities demonstrated the Indian capacity for education. The ordinary Britisher remained unaware of the volume of illiteracy which persisted in India, unremedied under British rule. There was, however, fair knowledge in Britain of the continuing strife between Hindus and Muslims in India, of the danger of serious conflict if British rule were withdrawn. There was, until the end of the Second World War, no conception of how this problem might be basically solved by the creation of a Muslim 'Pakistan'. Despite the inter-communal tensions, in 1939 the Viceroy of India, Lord Linlithgow, formally stated on 17 October that 'Dominion status remained the objective of His Majesty's Government'.

Those of us who were in India before and during the War knew that provincial self-government from 1937 had worked well. The Indian National Congress had participated fully in it until the late autumn of 1939. We met, too, those educated young Indians, utterly friendly, yet bent on achieving Indian freedom from Britain in the nearest possible future. They were men strongly influenced by Gandhi but not converted by him to *ahimsa*. When, in 1942, British soldiers in Poona and Ahmednagar received Gandhi and Nehru and other Congress leaders into our care after their arrest, we were impressed not by Gandhi's planned civil disobedience campaign but by the appalling outbreaks of violence all over India that followed those arrests. Government buildings were set on fire. Police stations and post offices were attacked; these were the chief targets. Five hundred and fifty railway stations were destroyed.

Railway lines were damaged, and there were twenty-four derailments of trains. An airport was attacked, a grand trunk road cut at various places, boats on the Hooghly River sunk, petrol stations in New Delhi set on fire.[12] All of us feared to travel by train, and even Army Chaplains were armed if they went shopping on foot in Poona.

There were 27,000 prisoners in Bihar gaols.[13] Gandhi wrote to the Viceroy to say that 'Of course, I deplore the happenings that have taken place since 9 August past.'[14] The number of British troops in India, so badly needed for the Japanese War, had to be increased for the maintenance of order and internal communications. The soldiers saw enough to persuade them that the British were not wanted in India. If they went to Indian cinemas they were impressed by the ostentatious exodus of young Indians during the playing of 'God save the King'. After the end of the War, there was a strike of naval ratings in Bombay and Karachi; on 17 February 1946 there was a mutiny in the Royal Indian Navy. British rule in India was rushing towards its end, its continuance wanted by nobody. H. V. Hodson, a former Constitutional Adviser to the Viceroy, tells us that 'Indian political consciousness had increased', that 'the subject people' had 'become imbued with the ideas of the governing race'.[15] An Indian writes:

It is widely believed in this country and abroad that India won her freedom from British Imperialism through the struggle waged in the form of non-co-operation and civil disobedience, commonly known as *satyagraha* initiated by Mahatma Gandhi.

He goes on:

India became free on August 15 1947 ... It has been maintained by historians that India became free through the non-violent struggle conducted by the Congress ... Even if it were conceded that the 1942 movement was a non-violent movement, the fact remains that by 1944 there was nothing left of that movement.[16]

A Labour Government was returned to power in Britain in 1945 under Clement Attlee, a Prime Minister inclined on principle towards Indian independence, 'dedicated to the ideals of self-determination and partnership'.[17] He had agreed that 'we need a man to do in India what Durham did in Canada'. This was before Gandhi's last civil disobedience campaign.[18] The man he needed in 1946 was at hand: Admiral Lord Mountbatten of Burma.

There was a nation behind the Prime Minister ready enough to go along with him. Respect for Mr Gandhi was almost universal. But those who came to power in India in 1947 were those who, with the new Prime Minister, J. K. Nehru, had been prepared to use non-violence and violence alike in their struggle for freedom. Gandhi's personal influence (rather than his civil disobedience campaigns) had promoted that successful struggle against the British which included the use of all sorts of methods and weapons which Gandhi abhorred. He himself was not happy with the independence won in 1947. Statues, photographs, drawings and paintings of him are to be seen in public places throughout India. They are all part of the legend.

Gandhi and his 'passive resistance' methods inspired others, notably Martin Luther King in the United States of America. Martin Luther King Jnr, of Atlanta, Georgia, was 'electrified' in his student days by the message of Gandhi. He thought of him as 'one of the great men of all time', 'probably the first person in history to lift the love ethic of Jesus above mere interaction between individuals to a powerful effective social force on a large scale'.[19] M. L. King was born in 1929, the son of the Revd Martin Luther King Snr, of Ebenezer Baptist Church, in a middle-class area of black Atlanta. His father had taken a doctorate of divinity degree at Morris Brown College in Atlanta, and had a church with a membership of several thousand. Young Martin enrolled at Morehouse College, Atlanta, at the age of fifteen and studied sociology. In 1944, at the age of nineteen, he went on to Crozer Seminary, Pennsylvania, to study for his BA in Divinity. He proceeded to Boston University for his doctorate. He took courses also at Harvard, across the Charles River. Even before he gained his PhD, he was chosen to be pastor of Ebenezer Baptist Church, Montgomery, Alabama. When the troubles began in Montgomery in 1955 he began to take Gandhi really seriously. On 5 December 1955, he was elected president of the Montgomery Improvement Association. He had become, hesitatingly, a convinced and convincing anti-segregationist. He had really at last come to believe that 'all men are created equal'.

It was George Wallace, who was to become Governor of Alabama in 1962, who had declared, 'I say, segregation now! Segregation tomorrow! Segregation for ever!'[20] The fight was on now to secure that black passengers on Montgomery buses had equal rights with whites for seats on the buses. A boycott of the buses by the blacks had begun. That evening, Dr King appealed for protest, not violence, for people 'to protest courageously but with dignity and Christian love'.[21] The boycott persisted, despite its inconvenience to the black people. On 27 January 1956, King had an experience in his kitchen in the course of which he believed that he heard the voice of Jesus telling him to persevere. 'Stand up for righteousness. Stand up for justice. Stand up for truth,' said the voice.[22] On 27 February, a white official of the Fellowship of Reconciliation explained to him 'how the essence of non-violence was a refusal to retaliate against evil, a refusal based on the realization that "the law of retaliation is the law of the multiplication of evil"'.[23]

Despite bitter white opposition, the boycott succeeded. After arrests of blacks and bombings by whites, after great meetings of black supporters of the boycott and the formation of the Southern Negro Leaders Conference (SNLC), on 18 December 1956 the Mongomery City Lines buses were desegregated. King had become a national figure. He claimed to have awakened a 'sense of shame within the oppressor'; he added that 'the end is reconciliation ... the creation of the beloved community'.[24]

Bayard Rustin, an experienced white co-worker, whose past included brief membership of the Young Communist League, remarked that King had begun to develop 'a decidedly Gandhi-like view'; Richard Smiley noted that King at first used the phrase 'passive resistance' instead of 'non-violence'.[25] However, the non-violent battle was only just beginning. Literary tests were preventing blacks throughout the South from receiving their voting rights. The truth was that Southern whites tended to regard their black fellow-citizens as inferior beings needing to be kept in their place. These were, after all, the States where slavery had been abolished less than a hundred years before. I myself was brought up in a Kentucky town where 'niggers' were treated kindly but with condescension. I remember that the great fear as far back as the 1920s was that an in-coming Republican Government might desegregate the schools. It did nothing of the kind. The blacks naturally had their own schools in 'Niggertown'. After the Republican victory, they kept them.

King's anti-segregation campaign was waged more than thirty years later. He led the fight for integrated schooling not only in the South but in those places like Chicago where it also did not exist. He led it for equal voting rights, for equality of opportunity in employment, for the right for blacks to eat and drink wherever whites ate and drank, for the desegregation of all parks and amusement facilities. He flew around the Southern States and up to the North too,

accompanied by fellow-leaders of the SNLC, holding meetings, organizing protests, leading marches. He achieved a
relationship with President John Kennedy after his election in
1960, and with his brother Robert Kennedy, the Attorney
General. The Kennedy brothers of Massachusetts had been
ignorant of the problems of the Southern blacks, rather than
prejudiced against them. Robert Kennedy declared: 'I haven't
known many Negroes in my life.'[26] On 11 June 1963,
President Kennedy went on television, calling on the American
people to 'banish segregation and racism from the land'. On
28 August, a 'march on Washington' culminated at the
Lincoln Memorial with a speech from Dr King. There were
probably two hundred thousand people present, and nearly
25% were white.[27] Virginia, one of the Southern States, was
just across the Potomac River. The tradition of the Confederate
slavery States was beginning to perish. Martin Luther King
spoke of his dream:

> I have a dream that one day this nation will rise up and live
> out the true meaning of its creed – we hold these truths to
> be self-evident, that all men are created equal.

'Let freedom ring', he said, 'from every hill and mole hill of
Mississippi. From every mountain top, let freedom ring.'
Professor David Garrow writes:

> Although he did not know it, the speech had been the
> rhetorical achievement of a lifetime, the clarion call that
> conveyed the moral power of the movement's cause to the
> millions who had watched the live national network
> coverage.[28]

King and his followers went on to sandwiches with the
President in the White House. Earlier in the year, on 11 June,
the University of Alabama at Tuscaloosa was de-segregated,

over the glumly protesting presence of the State Governor, George Wallace. The United States Deputy Attorney General was there to see the duly mobilized National Guard march in as two black students were admitted to the university. By 1988 there were 1,750 black students in the university, and ex-Governor Wallace is quoted as saying, 'I was wrong, I was wrong.' In 1964, Martin Luther King was awarded the Nobel Peace Prize.

His success was not yet complete, as he well knew. Yet he had won enough in the South and throughout the United States to guarantee almost complete success in the end. He had been physically assaulted with fist and with knife; he had been in gaol again and again. Over all this, he had triumphed, offering only non-violence in return for persecution. His reputation and his influence seem to have been little damaged by the weaknesses of his personal life. As he travelled around the country, staying in hotels, various women shared his bed. Many of his nights in hotel rooms were 'bugged' by the Federal Bureau of Investigation. He ate heavily and sometimes drank with his companions until the early hours of the morning. He had a mistress whose flat was available for him in Atlanta itself (to which he had returned from Montgomery). He did not excuse himself, but declared that sexual intercourse was a form of relaxation.[29] Professor David Garrow, his most respected and objective biographer, described all this as 'King's compulsive sexual athleticism' (*New York Review*). In the same issue, C. Vann Woodward wrote that 'this most unwelcome information' was 'essential to any full and honest portrayal of King ... and to an adequate understanding of the threats under which he worked'. Not only his enemies but his friends and Presidents Kennedy and Johnson were well aware of his weaknesses. However, 'those who worked with King accepted this as an expression of both a cultural tradition and a demonstrative temperament'.[30] He never achieved that relaxation which he needed and sought. He suffered greatly from depression, and was continually complaining of tiredness.[31] He frequently referred to the possibility of an early death. He was only thirty-eight when he was assassinated at Memphis, Tennessee, on 4 April 1968. President Lyndon Johnson declared Sunday 7 April 'a day of national mourning'. Vice-President Hubert Humphrey, Robert Kennedy, Richard Nixon, Harry Belafonte, Jacqueline Kennedy and many others attended his funeral in Ebenezer Church, Atlanta.

He had won his fight for Negro rights by non-violent methods. He had made his appeal by his words and actions for justice for his fellow-blacks. The white American people to whom he had appealed had responded in the end favourably. Owing to the American tradition of freedom and the American system of compulsory education for all, an educated, freedom-loving people found it difficult to deny the justice for which he asked. It is difficult for those who have freedom themselves, and whose education has taught them to respect it, to continue indefinitely to tolerate the refusal of justice and freedom to others in their midst. Unlike Gandhi in his attempt to propagate *ahimsa* to his deprived and poorly educated fellow-Indians, Martin Luther King was appealing for justice to those who appreciated justice, to the literate and the free. His bust stands in the Capitol, and a national annual holiday honours regularly his name.

In a 1967 sermon, delivered on 30 April, at the time of King's opposition to the Vietnam War, he made it clear that he did not believe that non-violence would have been the right answer to the evil of Hitlerism. He said, 'If I had confronted the call to serve in military service in a war against Hitler, I believe that I would have probably temporarily sacrificed my pacifism because Hitler was such an evil force in history.'[32] Even amongst an educated people like the Germans, it was possible for evil to obtain such a hold that no opposition except that of force could move it. Peace-loving nations were driven to war with Hitlerism, and freedom-loving individuals to plan revolt and murder. Good people could see no other way. Amongst such good people was Dietrich Bonhoeffer. He himself, a peace-loving man, was much attracted to India and had been attracted to Mahatma Gandhi before the War. Bishop George Bell of Chichester had written to Gandhi in October 1934 to tell him that a 'young man, a German pastor in London ... a very good theologian, a most earnest man', wanted to come to him 'to study community life'.[33] Bonhoeffer was never able to come. Nor was he ever completely converted to *ahimsa*, although always a man of peace. It was as 'essentially a peaceable person' that I heard him described recently on the radio. He cared yet more deeply for justice. He was hanged for complicity in a murder plot in 1945.

Dietrich Bonhoeffer was born in Silesia, with his twin sister Sabine, in 1906 after his parents' five other children. His was a family of high social standing and liberal outlook, one with a tradition both of culture and of ethical integrity. All the children were taught consideration and gentleness towards one another. In that household everybody enjoyed music and everybody sang; Dietrich played the piano. His father, Dr Karl Bonhoeffer, became Professor of Psychiatry and Neurology in Berlin in 1912. In the family home in Breslau, and later in Berlin-Grunewald, Dietrich grew up a person of culture, goodness, charm, grace, 'a man of great stature ... very human, but a brilliant thinker'.[34] He chose, to his parents' surprise, to become a Lutheran theologian, a pupil of Adolf Harnack, a friend and admirer of Karl Barth. He lectured and preached, worked as an assistant pastor in Spain, and was ordained on 15 November 1931. He served from 1932 as an international secretary in the German Co-ordination Office for Ecumenical Youth Work. Whenever he spoke, people listened to him.

Indeed, with the coming to power in Germany of Adolf Hitler in January 1933, Bonhoeffer identified himself with the so-called 'Confessing Church', a body of Protestants in revolt against the subservience of the official German Church to the Nazi state. In the summer of 1934, the Confessing Church published its 'Barmen Declaration'. This asserted against the so-called 'German Christians' that there were no 'events, powers, images and truths' in divine revelation other than 'God's one Word'. Bonhoeffer became in 1935 director of one of the seminaries of the Confessing Church. It was at first located at Zingst on the Baltic coast, and then at Finkenwalde near Stettin. Here he made Eberhard Bethge his close friend and colleague. Bethge was a younger man, who became Bonhoeffer's biographer. Dietrich Bonhoeffer's influence, theologically, spiritually, culturally, upon most of his students was immense and enduring. The seminary had to be closed on 8 December 1937, in the course of the persecution of the Confessing Church by the Nazi Government.

In what Gordon Rupp has described as 'its noble utterance at Barmen' in 1934,[35] the Confessing Church had declared the Church's unqualified loyalty to Jesus Christ, recognizing his claim on the whole of human life and rejecting all other claims which might compete. The loyalty of Bonhoeffer to Christ and to God's Word dictated to him his opposition to Hitler and to the Nazi ideology. He was willing to make the Nazi salute when custom demanded it; but he was utterly unwilling to become subservient in his mind. After the terrible 'Kristallnacht' of anti-Jewish violence on 8 November 1938, 25,000 male Jews were rounded up and sent to concentration camps. With the outbreak of war in 1939, Bonhoeffer realized that there was now no conceivable end, perhaps for years, to Hitlerite injustice in Germany, to the persecution of the free, to the cruelty to the Jews, to the overrunning of other people's lands and liberties. From the time of Hitler's taking control of Hungary, for example, two-thirds of the Jews of that country were first enslaved, then destroyed. Bonhoeffer had to choose between standing by, and becoming involved in conspiracy against the Nazi Government. He made his choice, joining in a movement which would employ force to bring to an end at as early a date as possible a régime of violence, injustice, war. He chose himself to become an activist in violence, rather than to remain a spectator. In claiming that force was on this occasion necessary, he was not, of course, asserting that the end justifies the means. Rather, he was demonstrating that this was one of those rare occasions when loyalty to Jesus Christ demanded that one at least of his laws, the commandment against killing, needed to be broken. It was to this kind of thinking that he had laboriously worked his way from the conventional morality of both Judaism and German Lutheranism. He remembered that his saviour had been accused of law-breaking in his attitude to the sabbath. Morality was in fact not cut and dried; faithfulness was more than and different from law-keeping. He was able to explain himself in writing only to a limited extent, for most of his writing was done under the Nazi tyranny. His dedicated life testified to his faith. Those who knew him and those who have written of him seem to have accepted the rightness for him of participating at that time in conspiracy and violence in a 'boundary situation'.[36] Those who believe that it was right for Dietrich Bonhoeffer to agree to involve himself in a plot to kill must be prepared to consider the possibility of other Christians at other times becoming rightly involved in the use of life-taking force when gross injustice is being committed.

It is difficult for those who did not know Hitler's Germany from 1933 to 1945 to understand the extent and the depth of the injustice that went on there and also the determination of the Nazis to hold on to power. There were new and terrible developments of this power during the year 1939 when Bonhoeffer was introduced by his distinguished brother-in-law Hans Dohnanyi to the conspiracy against Hitler. This was based upon the Abwehr, the élite headquarters of the German counter-espionage system. Dohnanyi challenged Bonhoeffer as to how 'all they that take the sword shall perish by the sword' (Matt. 26.52). Bonhoeffer accepted the challenge, replied that the warning was indeed valid, that there was 'need of such men as will accept its validity for themselves'.[37] He wrote:

> We have been silent witnesses of evil deeds; we have been drenched by many storms; we have learnt the art of equivocation and pretence; experience has made us suspicious of others and kept us from being truthful and open; intolerable conflicts have worn us down and even made us cynical ... Will our inward power of resistance be strong enough, and our honesty with ourselves remorseless enough, for us to find our way back to simplicity and straightforwardness?[38]

We must consider briefly but frankly to what extent he chose to become involved in the plot against Hitler. He declared, says Eberhard Bethge, that he was prepared personally to kill the Führer.[39] He was not, in fact, a good shot or an explosives expert. His rôle in the conspiracy at the Abwehr obliged him to lie and in various other ways to deceive, both before his arrest and especially after it (chiefly for the sake of his fellow-conspirators). He became an expert in the writing of letters intended to deceive his accusers. They were to proclaim his innocence and to help the plot on Hitler's life to go forward. For those who today know all this, Bonhoeffer in his Christian nobility remains above adverse criticism. He himself wrote:

> If I refuse to incur guilt against the principle of truthfulness for the sake of my friend, if I refuse to tell a robust lie for the sake of my friend ... if I refuse to bear guilt for charity's sake, then my action is in contradiction to my responsibility which has its foundation in reality. Here ... it is in the responsible acceptance of guilt that a conscience which is bound solely to Christ will best bear its innocence.[40]

Louie G. Hechanova, CSSR, reports him as having said of himself: 'All that is Christian in me protests against violence, and yet in the present circumstances I can do no other.'

All this must cause the Christian to think furiously. This gentle, peace-loving young theologian made his deliberate, conscientious choice. He knew, too, like more recent South American Christian revolutionaries (and others), that it is not enough to plan to destroy the bad régime, but that it is vitally necessary simultaneously to plan for the raising up and maintenance of the régime to take its place, one which is just and free and peace-creating. The *Freiburg Memorandum* of 1933 made plans for a future liberal order in Germany. It worked out the details of 'church policy, education, social and economic policy, and future peace'.[41] If the plot for the assassination of Hitler had succeeded, if Bonhoeffer's ideas conveyed to the British Government by his admiring friend George Bell, Bishop of Chichester, in 1942, had been heeded, the terrible war would have been shortened; the peace itself might have been better; thousands of lives would have been saved.

Dietrich Bonhoeffer was arrested on 5 April 1943, on the same day as the arrest of his sister Christine and his brother-in-law, Hans Dohnanyi. He had two years in various prisons. 'He personally never doubted the rightness of the course he had taken and the opening up of new insights.'[42] In the notorious concentration camp at Buchenwald he heard in the distance the sound of the liberating American guns from the Werra before he went to his death by hanging at Flossenburg, north of Passau, on 9 April 1945. It was Low Sunday; the Germans call it 'Quasimodo Sunday'. His bravery and his faith had impressed all who were with him during his captivity. The moral decisions which he made ought to impress all who have moral choices to make in the face of injustice. He had chosen to lie and was prepared to kill. Yet it was finely said of Bonhoeffer by one who pleaded for mercy for him:

His frankness and his love of truth in every situation were clearly unbounded ... His trust in and fearlessness before men derived in him from the same source: it was the rock-like conviction, which penetrated his whole being, of the reality and truth of 'justice'. The word had for him the gravest religious content.[43]

CHAPTER FOUR

Violence in Northern Ireland

In all political parties in Britain and in the two leading parties of the Republic of Ireland (irrespective of which of them is in power) there is condemnation of terrorism. Almost the whole British population condemns it, Irish Roman Catholic and Anglican bishops denounce it, politicians compete to describe it with such epithets as 'obscene'; those who practise it are 'pathological cases'. I wrote to a distinguished Irish Roman Catholic academic concerning the IRA and Sinn Fein. He replied briefly that the 'Provos' are led by evil men and that Sinn Fein is '90% based on murder'. I did not feel confidence in his capacity to make so sweeping a judgment. At a church question-and-answer session I tried to explain something of the minds of Sinn Fein members whom I knew. I noticed an elderly man physically quivering with rage, and one member of the congregation chose to tell me afterwards that he was sorry that I had come. It is not unreasonable to suggest that there may well be some prejudice behind all this; prejudice is often founded on ignorance and blinds to truth. I do not know how well eminent Irish ecclesiastics actually know members of the Provisional IRA and of Sinn Fein. I do know that many of the most prejudiced English know nothing whatsoever of Ireland and very little of the Irish. Even people who live on the western coast of Britain seldom bother to go over to Ireland (except, perhaps, like Scottish clergy friends of mine, for an afternoon's picnic). It is an unfortunate habit of English people who have never been to Ireland to lay down the law about it.

The late Sean MacBride, SC, formerly Secretary-General of the International Committee of Jurists, a holder of the Nobel Peace Prize and of seven honorary doctorates, has written from experience and with clarity of the British ignorance and prejudice concerning Ireland:

> The majority of the ordinary decent people of England are not really interested in what happens in Ireland. Their knowledge of Anglo-Irish relations is minimal. They have been taught to regard the Irish people as impossible and irrational, even if somewhat amusing and gifted. They could not care less as to what is happening in Ireland ... In their own country and in countries which they do not seek to dominate, the British are reasonable, fair-minded and even lovable. It is otherwise in areas which they regard as their preserve. In regard to Ireland the British government and establishment are just incapable of being objective, fair-minded or just.[1]

It is the charge of injustice towards some people in Northern Ireland which riles the British. They do not care for philosophy; for them 'justice' concerns law; and the law is being kept, broadly speaking. Justice, however, philosophically, means basically the treating of people with respect. There are many in the Roman Catholic minority in Northern Ireland, and amongst others too, who do not believe that Britain has always acted justly. Many Irish, strangely, tend to recall the Declaration Act of the Irish 'Patriot Parliament' of 1689, 'more representative of the majority of the nation than any other parliament'.[2] It resolved that the English Parliament should not legislate for Ireland. Its decisions were rendered void by the Battle of the Boyne, won by Danish, Dutch, German, French and English troops under a Dutch King of England. The Anglican theologian, Dr John Austin Baker, now Bishop of Salisbury, declared on 1 December 1980 that the present state of insecurity in Northern Ireland is the fault of Great Britain. He affirmed:

> England seized Ireland for its own military benefit; it planted Protestant settlers there to make it strategically secure; it humiliated and penalized the native Irish and their Catholic religion. And then, when it could no longer hold on to the whole island, kept back part to be a home for the settlers' descendants . . . Our injustice created the situation; and by constantly repeating that we will maintain it so long as the majority wish it, we actively inhibit Protestant and Catholic from working out a new future together. This is the root of violence.[3]

Decent young (and not so young) Irishmen have taken to violence in despair of getting justice through any other means. Their plea that under the present system they suffer injustice is not even heard, let alone acted on. The British Government does not, except on rare occasions, listen to those who feel so strongly that they resort to violence. David Apter, Professor of Comparative Political and Social Development at Yale University, gave a series of lectures in Oxford in early 1988 concerning his study over many years of terrorism and of men of violence in different countries. He was emphatic that terrorists are no more 'pathological cases' than any others with strong convictions. He declared that those who could see violence 'from the inside' would learn that the normal assumption that violent men are evil men is not valid. Only 'from the inside', he said, could terrorism be understood. From his world-wide study of terrorists, he had come to the conclusion that the terrorists he had met were actuated by principles. They were people concerned with situations which needed rectifying, and there would be no rectification unless force were used. He said that nobody could understand anti-Israeli violence on the part of Palestinians in the Gaza Strip unless he were himself a suffering and frustrated Palestinian. We in Britain and America are used to living under the rule of law; what we need is normally obtainable through legal and non-violent means, by democratic method and due process of law. In Northern Ireland and elsewhere, when democratic method and due process of law do not seem to many to provide what is just, they tend to turn to the damaging of property or of other people. There is an impatience, a refusal to wait indefinitely for justice which, it seems to them, will never otherwise come.

Professor Apter, in Japan and Latin America, in Germany and Italy, came to see that, in men of violence, 'vision and fear' often coalesced. The fear of continuing injustice, and the hope of justice that could still be, drove them towards the violence needed, as they thought, to uproot injustice and to plant justice in. When 'institutional mechanisms' would not deliver the goods, 'extra-institutional protest' had been bound to arise; this had led sometimes to terrorism. When you meet the terrorists, you begin, he says, to get over the normal Western assumption that violence is necessarily evil. He reminds us that all democratic reform has had some violence connected with it. Such struggles have bred both history and legend, and both have sometimes seemed to justify further violence. We English have had our Great Rebellion and our Glorious Revolution, neither of them without the use of force, and both commended in the history books.

Professor Apter writes that 'one of the more remarkable

findings of interviews with terrorists is how normal they seem to be, at least to outward appearances'. He compares what he finds of the high principles of the terrorists with the common impression that violence is 'a form of personal compensation, a settling of scores against society or authority', 'disturbing, dangerous, and aberrant, a kind of pathology'.[4] A prominent Northern Ireland politician in Belfast in July 1988 described Gerry Adams MP to me as 'just a murderer'. All who know Gerry Adams are aware that this is not a just description of him.

It is indeed impossible for United Kingdom citizens who have not been to and stayed in Ireland to understand the country and its people in the Republic and in so-called Ulster. The Englishman is inclined to blame the Irish for not being loyal Englishmen. The English as a whole are inclined to imagine that the Irish people, whose minds are shaped in a different environment and tradition, are just like the English across the sea but speak with a brogue. Even statesmen like William Ewart Gladstone and David Lloyd George, who at different times became convinced of the need of some sort of Home Rule for Ireland, had themselves scarcely been to the country. Gladstone, in fact, had been only once. He wrote to Hartington on 30 May 1885: 'I have never looked much in Irish matters at negotiation. . .'[5] He had never looked much at anything Irish. In 1885, he apologized in the House of Commons for the British treatment of Ireland. He described it as a 'broad and black blot' upon Britain's record. His fellow Liberals were for the most part as ignorant as he was of the Irish country and the Irish mind. Of Lloyd George, it was said that his 'views on Ireland, when he chose to have them, amounted to bored and resentful repulsion'.[6] He had no compelling urge to do anything for Ireland, in which he was uninterested. He had forgotten or perhaps he had never even heard of 'the hungry forties' of the previous century, when again and again the Irish potato crops failed. The potato was the staple food of the Irish people, to whom bread was unfamiliar and for whom grain was in short supply and expensive. Near Kilclooney on the Donegal coast in July 1988 the driver who was giving me a lift pointed out the place at sea where the British warship had turned away the ship from overseas bringing grain for the starving people. He said that this information had been passed on from generation to generation over the hundred and forty years since it had all happened. The famine had been terrible in its effects. 'Between 1846 and 1851 nearly a million persons emigrated, and ... roughly about a million and a half perished during the famine, of hunger, diseases brought on by hunger and fever.' 'The treatment of the Irish people by the British government during the famine has been described as "genocide-race murder"'. All this, and much more, was written by Cecil Woodham-Smith, after long and thorough research. She concludes with reference to the famine: 'The history of what then occurred is deeply engraved on the memory of the Irish race; all hope of assimilation with England was then lost, and bitterness without parallel took possession of the Irish mind.' She wrote that at the end of 1849 'there were about a million destitute in the workhouses and on relief, and ... Sydney Godolphin Osborne frequently saw dead bodies lying by the side of the road.' In the midst of the starvation, during the six months between August 1849 and the end of January 1850, nearly 7000 people were evicted from their homes in the Kilrush, Co. Clare, region alone. 'The famine left hatred behind. Between Ireland and England the memory of what was done and endured has lain like a sword.'[7]

An historian comments: 'So it was that the rulers of Ireland rarely, if ever, visited it, never saw its miseries, never experienced themselves the people's sense of injustice, nor comprehended their resentment at remedies concocted by those who had not troubled to acquire first-hand knowledge of the disease.'[8] To go to Northern Ireland or to the Republic is to go amongst people with different backgrounds and sentiments. The Englishman may find himself in material comfort but intellectually and spiritually not at home. If he chooses to 'speak out' loudly on Northern Irish matters, as Northern Ireland Secretaries tend to do, he reveals himself as one who does not understand. The English traveller may go to Northern Ireland, indeed to Belfast itself, and see and hear nothing of significance. It depends upon where he goes and to whom he speaks. He may leave his comfortable English-style hotel and find himself ill-at-ease in some of the streets of Belfast in an environment different from anything he has ever previously experienced. He may never have heard of the declaration of Easter 1916 of 'the Provisional Government of the Irish Republic'. It proclaims 'the rights of the people of Ireland to the ownership of Ireland'. It places 'the cause of the Irish Republic under the protection of the Most High God'. It occupies a place of honour in the Bullingdon Arms, Oxford, where Irish and English meet to drink. It was the symbol of a small Irish revolt in which the General Post Office in Dublin was temporarily seized. This was mercilessly crushed; all seven of the signatories of the declaration were tried and shot. Their names were Thomas J. Clarke, Sean MacDiarmada, P. H. Pearse, James Connolly, Thomas McDonagh, Eamonn Ceannt, Joseph Plunket. The wounded James Connolly was carried on a stretcher to the firing squad. An historian writes:

> The government's reaction to rebellion in war-time ... ignored the lessons of Irish history and initiated a decisive shift in Irish opinion... Execution transformed the rebel leaders into martyrs for Irish freedom.[9]

They are by no means forgotten. Roy Hattersley rightly says that 'the Irish have an obsession with their history'. The English do not, and do not understand those who do.

On Sunday morning, 14 December 1980, I walked from the

Anglican Franciscan house in Deerpark Road, along Crumlin Road into the city of Belfast and back. In the barricaded Catholic area, there were huge anti-British paintings on the sides of the houses. Hundreds of flags of the Irish Republic, at that time illegal, flew challengingly from the roof-tops. The street was empty. A man ran out to me. 'What's up?' he asked. I replied that to the best of my knowledge nothing was 'up'. He did not look reassured. There were anti-Royal Ulster Constabulary slogans up everywhere. Further on, there were anti-Nationalist threats on pillar-boxes in a Protestant area. When I returned to the Friary that morning, one of the Irish Brothers asked me where I had been. When I told him that I had walked into the city and back, he said that he would not have dared to do that. It had not previously occurred to me that I had done anything very brave or rash.

It was quite a different sort of scene in the Falls Road on Friday morning, 27 November 1987. The people were out shopping, the children on their way to school. The schools were to start at 11 a.m. that day. There was uncollected garbage. About 10.50 a.m. the soldiers came up the road in battle dress in single file at the double, stopping simultaneously at regular intervals. Each raised his rifle and aimed deliberately across the road. Then he doubled on to repeat the performance again and again. I watched in fascinated amazement, feeling that I must be dreaming or watching television or at the cinema. This could not be really going on in a city of the United Kingdom at the end of 1987. The shoppers just looked away in contempt, acting as if this were not happening. The soldiers themselves were mostly small; they looked very young, eighteen or nineteen perhaps, camouflaged, wooden-faced, trying seemingly not to think of what they were doing. I have learnt since that the exercise is part of the training to prepare soldiers to deal with 'renegades' and to 'respond to attack'. It is commonly called 'stop and seek' (stop dead and seek a target). I had been told, mistakenly, that the Royal

Ulster Constabulary had resumed its proper functions, 'taken over' from the Army. I saw no sign of this in the Falls Road in 1987 or 1988. This exercise must have made impressions on the unconscious minds of children, perhaps even on women shoppers. It keeps on surging up unasked into my own consciousness. I had been in Hitler's Germany and Mussolini's Italy, seen the tall Blackshirts on parade outside the Nazi Brown House in Munich. But I had never before seen or felt what I saw and felt in the Falls Road in Belfast that Friday morning. I saw young soldiers again, this time in smaller numbers, marching in single file along the Falls Road on the morning of 30 June 1988. Again they aimed their rifles in their exercise in intimidation. It seemed to me that these young soldiers could not care much for this exercise. I am told by one of their officers that most of them are 'philosophical' concerning their obviously unwanted presence in this part of Belfast. Indeed they themselves have been told that there is more likelihood of their being killed in the course of 'overseas service' than in Northern Ireland. More casualties occur in the locally recruited Ulster Defence Regiment than amongst the British forces stationed in Northern Ireland. Some of the latter serve there for only six months, some for as much as two years. The Ulster Defence Regiment is 90% non-Roman Catholic in composition.

I had come the previous morning, 29 June, from the Springhill Community in Springhill Avenue. Their house was one of the gaunt relics of a devastated area, not altogether easy to find, entered by its back door rather than its front. The Community had been founded in 1975 by Fr Des Wilson, a dedicated but independent-minded Roman Catholic priest. A relationship with his bishop, impaired for some years, has now been restored. Here at 123 Springhill Avenue was a resource and educational centre for teenagers alienated from their more regimented schools. Here the boys and girls, smiling and relaxed, strangely matured, came in about 9 a.m.

for their O-level lessons. Here in this house were Catholics believing passionately in the need of their fellow Irish for full development in an area where unemployment was running at over 50%, perhaps at 70%. Nearby was the Old Conway Street Flax Spinning Mill, where an extensive 'Project' was organized by the Community. There in the Conway Street complex is an Education Centre; there are Workers' Educational Association classes, lessons for the unemployed in O-level English and Psychology and Sociology and Mathematics, in A-level English Literature and Mathematics, in Political Studies and Philosophy, in pre-GCE Irish. Here also there is weaving, and there are attempts at job creation. There are cheap good midday meals for the unemployed and their wives, efforts to minister to and help political prisoners' wives. The Springhill Community is a registered charity, and as such it had at first received funding from various charitable trusts. Most of this funding has ceased; the Project was refused assistance from the Local Education Development Unit, despite the education and the training, on the instruction of the Northern Ireland Secretary. Springhill, Conway Street, were condemned as 'politically orientated' because their organizers cared desperately for justice, for opportunity for the deprived, the under-privileged. Those who care deeply tend to express their convictions with tongue and pen. That is the way of democracy; it caused these good people, and the training, to be refused funding.

There is an alternative in Northern Ireland to that deeply caring, strongly expressed conviction of the need for remedying the ills of the under-privileged, which is sometimes branded as 'political involvement'. That alternative is a terrible silence and an attempted thoughtlessness. I encountered it at a trade union conference at Coleraine to which I went after leaving Belfast in November 1987. There was genuine friendliness and much luxury for a small sum at our hotel. For dinner on the Saturday night we had four different sorts of meat on our large plates. I remembered uncomfortably a picture I had seen in the Falls Road on the day before of a woman showing her children some joints in a butcher's shop window. 'People cook and eat those,' she was saying to the wide-eyed boy and girl. I said quietly to my neighbour that I had met some Sinn Fein people; quickly and decisively he whispered to me to keep quiet. The next day I mentioned that I had seen the soldiers exercising on the streets of Belfast. This time my neighbour nudged me with his knee. He came from Enniskillen. To a tall, highly intelligent young trade unionist I mentioned that no one seemed prepared to talk about some very real parts of Northern Ireland life. He replied rather sadly that people had learnt neither to think nor to speak. This prohibition, however imposed, upon the right (and duty) of members of various denominations among a group of trade union members to speak of matters concerning their area of the United Kingdom seemed, and seems, to me to be unbearable. Free thought and speech did not exist. A Sister said to me: 'It's all right to speak so long as you say nothing.' I went home unsatisfied. I had been warned long ago in Nazi Germany and Fascist Italy to take care of what I said, but I simply had not expected to find a similar ban within a so-called democracy. There is obviously something amiss, much that needs to be put right if real democracy is to be created.

There are many within Northern Ireland who inevitably find this conspiracy of silence even more unbearable than a mere English traveller did. So it is that men and women have come to conclude that the armed English presence which provokes and supports it must at all costs be removed. Where people speak most freely, in Sinn Fein, in the Falls Road, there seemingly the Armed Forces are most evident. There is, of course, more to the movement than this; there is the whole problem of injustice, of discrimination against the large Roman Catholic minority in the Province. Her Majesty's Stationery Office published in October 1987, under the Royal

Arms, a *Report on Religious and Political Discrimination* in Northern Ireland. It was drawn up by the Standing Advisory Commission on Human Rights. The Commission 'strongly supported' the need for 'urgent changes to be made to the law in the field of fair employment', declaring that there are 'pressing issues of social and economic concern at the present time'. Discrimination in employment against Roman Catholics is clearly illustrated in the *Report*. In the Northern Ireland Civil Service, for example, only one third of the jobs in general service grades were held by Roman Catholics[10] in a population in which 40% were Roman Catholics. Unemployment of Roman Catholics in similar groups of skilled workers aged 25–44 in the Ballymena area was 24.3%, compared with 12.7% for non-Romans.[11] The *Report* sums up: 'A man's religion is consistently shown to be a major determinant of his chance of being unemployed.'

There has been in the past gross discrimination in the allocation of housing by Protestant-controlled Councils. Lord Fitt, formerly Gerry Fitt, of the Social Democratic Labour Party, remembers with anger the allocation of a three-bedroomed house in an over-crowded area to a single woman, Emily Beattie, a Protestant. Even now he describes housing as 'the central means of discrimination against Catholics'.[12] It may well surprise us to read in the report of the Policy Studies Institute arranged for and recommended by the Commission on Human Rights that there is 'very little support for the idea that "discrimination" is the main problem'.[13] Yet the Commission recommends that 'substantial inequalities ... must be tackled as a matter of urgency'.[14] Discrimination in the past and present has helped to give Roman Catholic citizens a sense that they are 'second-class', that Government and Protestant majority are biassed against them. The Anglo-Irish Agreement of 1985 is dedicated towards the elimination of such bias. Fr Des Wilson believes that there can be no such elimination so long as the British remain in Northern Ireland

45

to prop up the Protestant majority. Not all Protestants are Paisleyites; many believe that they themselves must help in the removal of bias. The Catholic community, however, has become embittered; the flying of the flag of the Republic is a sign that some have lost all respect for the British connection. More than two and a half thousand people have been killed in Northern Ireland since the Civil Rights marches signalled a revival of 'the Troubles' in the 1960s. Scars have been left on minds.

Fr Wilson writes that the police are prejudiced against Roman Catholics, that the rejection of duly elected Sinn Fein councillors by other politicians is 'spurious, undemocratic and dishonest'.[15] He sees no hope under British rule for a party like Sinn Fein, 'reborn out of the conflicts in the poorest parts' of the country, and proclaiming 'the need for a Socialist Republic'.[16] He writes that courts fail to dispense justice, that the police 'attack rather than defend'.[17] For a responsible Christian person to make such charges there must be some ground. They need to be taken seriously, thoroughly investigated and debated. It is undemocratic that a terrible silence like that of the trade unionists should be the unwritten rule in Coleraine (and no doubt elsewhere).

I have heard Gerry Adams, President of Sinn Fein, deploring injuries to 'the innocent'. He was brought up in Abercorn Street North, in the Falls Road district. Soldiers and police seemed to him as he grew up to be instruments of injustice in Northern Ireland. At Springhill I met Joe Reid, and at Sinn Fein in the Falls Road I heard Tom Hartley patiently explaining to me how 'politically orientated' Roman Catholics inevitably feel. It is violence in the British, they say, that begets violence in them. A lot of Irish blood, they say, has been spilt in the streets of Derry and Belfast and in the fields of Armagh and Tyrone. On 'Bloody Sunday', 30 January 1972, fourteen unarmed civil rights demonstrators were killed by British paratroopers in Londonderry. The

Londonderry Coroner described this as 'sheer unadulterated murder'. On 11 November 1982, three unarmed terrorists were killed by the RUC who fired 109 shots into their car. In 1974, Fr Denis Faul and Fr Raymond Murphy, two respected priests, published their *British Army and Special Branch RUC Brutalities*.[18] Thirty cases of maltreated men were described in detail, some cases being corroborated by doctors. Men under interrogation, some as young as sixteen and seventeen, had been struck in their stomachs, hit with batons on their heads and in their private parts, kicked between the legs, stretched over electric fires. The late Bobby Sands gave an account of *One Day in My Life*[19] during his imprisonment, one of sustained cruelty. If conditions have improved, *Magilligan – A Cause for Concern*,[20] produced in 1987, gives examples of psychological pressure, strip-mirror searching of bodies, humiliation of prisoners and of their visiting relatives, isolation and harassment of many, all in an atmosphere 'dense with hate' at Magilligan Prison. A Sinn Fein poster shows women protesting against the use of plastic bullets by the RUC. 'Plastic bullets kill', says a placard held by sad but defiant nationalist mothers.

It seems easier for the English to forget or neglect such facts of life and death than for the Catholic Northern Irish. They remind me of an Irishman sentenced to thirty years' imprisonment for the possession of a rifle, and they tell me of the five military bases which surround the Catholic district of Ballymurphy. No one, they say, listens to their complaints, and the garbage remains uncollected. The emigration figures, says Tom Hartley, are appalling, worse than those of the previous century. Forty per cent, republicans claim, of the people of Northern Ireland are virtually debarred by an inadequate electoral system from having any real say in their own government. Tom called it 'a degradation of democracy'. In West Belfast were people, it seemed to me, who were thoughtful and caring, who knew a good deal about their own people, and whom the British authorities were presently unwilling to listen to because of their failure to denounce violence. I am referring to Sinn Fein. Tom Hartley said 'the British in Ireland only did anything when they were forced into doing it'. 'Until all are free, all are imprisoned,' said Joe Reid. Republicans were concerned with people and how people might become real people, thinking, listening, working out solutions to their very real problems. How different all this was from the silence of Coleraine. They supported violence because they could see no other way forward towards democracy for the Northern Irish. Those I have met and eaten and drunk with were thoughtful people, seemingly not unkindly.

Sinn Fein is often described in the press as 'the political wing of the Provisional Irish Republican Army'. Sinn Fein received 83,000 votes in the Northern Ireland local elections in 1987. The Provisional IRA is an illegal body, illegal in the Republic as well as in Northern Ireland. The Provisional IRA was set up at the end of 1969. Its members believe that only by means of violence can the British be persuaded to leave Northern Ireland. It, therefore, works by violent methods, the leadership being sometimes out of touch with local sections because of difficulties of communication between illegal bodies. 'Some units, especially in the rural areas, did not have any contact with the Army Council or the representatives of the GHQ staff for six months at a time.'[21] Because its activities are sometimes necessarily localized, there is much of the clumsiness of amateurs about some of its explosions. The Enniskillen bombing of 8 November 1987 seems to have been intended for the security forces who should have searched the area before the Remembrance Sunday ceremony. 'The IRA bombing teams were under a general instruction to avoid killing innocent civilians.'[22] On the other hand, 'anyone who wore the Queen's uniform was eligible for attack, whether he was a private soldier from the south of England or a

Protestant farmer who happened to be a part-time member of the Ulster Defence Regiment'.[23] The Birmingham public house bombing of 21 November 1973 (like the later 'Harrods' bombing of 1983) seemed to negate all that. 'Birmingham' resulted in the killing of twenty-one people and the injuring of one hundred and sixty-two. Of the Enniskillen bombing Gerry Adams declared that 'no one in the IRA would attempt to defend it'. He added that 'it was a mistake, it was wrong' and that it reinforced the need for the IRA to accept its responsibility for the safety of civilians.[24] At the Oxford Union on 5 March 1987 I heard Gerry Adams say: 'I have never, never, never, never supported civilian fatalities at any time.' The IRA bomb in a bus in July 1988 seems to have been intended for the Reservist driver before he picked the children up. The East Tyrone brigade of the IRA declared on 24 November 1988 that 'the IRA has nothing to gain by the deaths of civilians and in fact has much to lose in terms of support'.[25] The IRA does unashamedly kill judges, politicians and civil servants, whom it regards as instruments of oppression and injustice. The Bishop of Oxford commends Robert Tabor's argument that 'the purposes of a revolutionary force' is 'not to win victories but to stay in existence'. He continues: 'By staying in existence and posing a threat, a revolutionary army forces the government to spend an ever increasing amount of money on military measures. It seeks to be a continuing nuisance, whilst at the same time carrying out a propaganda war.' He quotes Tabor: 'The revolutionary principle bears repetition: The object ... is not to win battles, but to avoid defeat, not to end the war, but to prolong it, until political victory, more than battlefield victory, has been won.'[26] The IRA, and many others, believe that the British electorate is becoming ready for withdrawal from Northern Ireland.

Members of the IRA are often spoken of in Britain as 'evil men'. This is because they aim to kill; they frequently in fact kill the innocent. They may well be blamed for carelessness, clumsiness, the faults of the inexperienced who lack the expertise which more co-ordinated direction from head-quarters might have given them. There seems to be a lack of bitterness amongst them. One of them in an interview said: 'I don't see the man, only the uniform.'[27] 'Those that I fight I do not hate,' said W. B. Yeats' Irish airman. Civilians indeed die, as they all too frequently die in war. Those in the Armed Forces who kill them in war are not normally branded as 'evil'. Those who serve in the IRA believe that they are at war with the British forces and all who enforce British rule in Northern Ireland. Men like Bobby Sands and the nine other hunger strikers who died with him as a result of starving themselves to death in prison were not vicious criminals, but men of ideas and ideals. The Englishman finds all this difficult to believe. Brendan McFarlane, who organized the hunger strike in the Long Kesh Prison, was a devout Catholic of considerable spiritual power. He wrote on 31 July 1981: 'I've always understood why we need a big sacrifice to shift the Brits.'[28] The sacrifice of ten young lives was in process of being offered. One hesitates to use the word 'evil' of persons who have shown themselves capable of self-sacrifice. Danny Morrison at the graveside of Tom McElwee, one of the hunger-strikers, told the assembled company that the dead man had longed for Catholic-Protestant unity. He added that he did not claim certainty of God's blessing on their work, but that he did believe that 'there can never be any moral wrong in an oppressed people using force against their oppressors'.[29] All that is debatable. At least it shows that we are not dealing with a gang of vicious, thoughtless, merciless killers. My respected friend, Canon Bill Arlow of Belfast Cathedral, at the time Assistant Secretary of the Irish Council of Churches, helped to arrange a meeting in December 1974 with repre-sentatives of the IRA. He thought, he said, that he was 'going to meet a group of mindless monsters'. He found that some of them were temperate men, that they were 'men concerned about their children and men concerned about their church ... not the monsters I thought them to be'.[30] He confirmed this to me personally in June 1988.

Fr Des Wilson believes that it is a moral duty to remove the root cause of injustice in Northern Ireland, the British Government, and to replace it by a modern democratic government of the Irish people's own choosing.[31] Paul Johnson, the journalist, now a keen supporter of the Thatcher Government, once wrote:

> In Ireland over the centuries, we have tried every possible formula: direct rule, indirect rule, genocide, apartheid, puppet parliaments, real parliaments, martial law, civil law, colonization, land reform, partition. Nothing has worked. The only solution we have not tried is absolute and unconditional withdrawal.[32]

It is certain that all over Britain many people from all parties believe that it would be good for the British to withdraw, provided that it could be assured that 'a blood-bath', terrible inter-sectarian violence, would not immediately occur. Fr Wilson asserts that the militant Protestants 'have never fought in Ireland without the State's armed forces'.[33] It is a possibility that, if the British withdrew, the great silent majority of those who 'neither think nor speak' might come to life in the cause of peace. There might be a learning to live together. Roy Hattersley has remarked on what he has seen in Ireland, and I myself have noted it in the South: 'the tenderness which suddenly overcomes the old enmities'.[34]

I heard Mr Charles Haughey, Taoiseach of the Irish Republic, speak at the J. F. Kennedy School of Political Science at Harvard on 26 April 1988. With great care and moderation he talked of a reasonable chance of the different Parties in the North and the South of Ireland beginning to talk together. Gerry Adams has spoken recently concerning the impossibility for the moment of a 'military solution'. Dr Conor Cruise O'Brien has written of a 'faith in the possibility of defeating terrorism ... wearing thin'.[35] *The Irish Post* of 30 April 1988 tells of a resolution of the annual conference of the Association of Cinematography and Television Technicians which called for a British withdrawal from Ireland. 'Britain', it said, 'can play no progressive role in Ireland.'[36] It went on to support 'the right of national self-determination for the Irish people' and to pledge itself in favour of 'the immediate withdrawal of British troops'. These are straws in the wind. There are various Irish folk who have assured me that the militants will 'think again' when the British withdraw. In the meantime Gerry Adams and others are already thinking again. Violence may not now be the way to freedom; hard thinking about the future of a free united Ireland certainly is. In a home in the Bogside from which there have been imprisonments, I spent two afternoons in July 1988 as people came and went. All talked of how the best possible future for Ireland might come to be. 'As for the Government,' says my Conservative hairdresser, as he clips away at the little that is left, 'they'll have to get round the table and talk.' He never spoke a more true and significant word.

On 28 January 1989 at Sinn Fein's annual conference at the Mansion House in Dublin, Gerry Adams condemned 'those operations in which civilians are killed'. He said that he was ready for talks with any of the parties 'in an effort to secure justice and peace'.[37] Martin McGuinness, closely identified with the IRA, supported him, 'because the killing of civilians is wrong'.[38] The 'Banshee' unit of the IRA responsible for the Enniskillen killings was finally disbanded at the same time.[39] In a leading article on 5 February 1989, *The Observer* declared that 'all parties inch forward from positions in which they have been frozen for decades'.

CHAPTER FIVE

Palestine, South Africa, Central and South America

Before the First World War, the Jews were in a small minority in Palestine. In 1880, there were 20,000 Jews in the country, comprising 5% of the population.[1] However, immigration of Jews into Palestine increased at the end of the nineteenth century and during the first fourteen years of the twentieth century. Jews who had owned only 2% of the land in 1880 found landowners willing enough to sell land to them. Zionism became a strong political movement with the writing of Theodor Herzl (1860–1904). His *Jewish State* was published in 1896. The first Zionist Congress was held in Basle in August 1897. The Congress committed the movement to the colonization of Palestine. Israel Zangwill's romantic picture of this was of 'a people without land going to a land without people'. This was no true picture. Arabs had come to Palestine in the seventh century AD, inter-married with the local Palestinian people, and helped to make it part of the Islamic Empire. These Palestinians constituted the basic population under the Turks before the War of 1914–18. As a result of various pressures towards the end of that War, Mr A.

J. Balfour, the British Foreign Secretary, expressed support in his famous Declaration of 2 November 1917 for the creation in Palestine of a 'National Homeland' for the Jewish people. In this Declaration he asserted blandly, but no doubt sincerely, that 'nothing shall be done which may prejudice the civil and religious rights of non-Jewish communities in Palestine'. The *Jewish Chronicle* declared this to be 'a triumph for civilization and humanity'. Under the Mandate for Palestine conferred on Britain by the League of Nations in 1922, Jewish immigrants in limited numbers were allowed into Palestine. Many Jews were smuggled illegally into the country. By 1944, there were 508,000 Jews in Palestine, together with 1,222,000 Palestinians. A United Nations partition plan in 1947, after the Second World War, proposed a partition of the land, with a Jewish state which would include half a million Jews and with a roughly similar number of Palestinians occupying between 50% and 60% of the territory of Palestine. This was generous provision for the Jews who comprised only 31% of the population and occupied only 6% of the land. However, the actual settlement of 1948, one created by the violence of war, was far more favourable. In that year, the British had given up their Mandate on 14 May and moved out. The Jews set up their own state of Israel, defeated a joint attack on them by the Arab powers and found themselves in possession of 77% of the land of Palestine. 'Some 900,000 Palestinians were rendered homeless or stateless.'[2] David Ben-Gurion, first Prime Minister of the state of Israel, declared in his introduction to *The History of the Haganah*:

In our country there is room only for Jews. We will say to the Arabs: 'Move over.' If they are not in agreement, if they resist, we will push them by force.[3]

As a result of the 1967 'Six Day War', the state of Israel found itself firmly in possession of the 'West Bank' of the Jordan

River including the Old City of Jerusalem, of the Gaza Strip on the Mediterranean coast, and of the Golan Heights, north of Galilee. It proceeded to annex East Jerusalem, and in December 1981, the Golan Heights; it administered the West Bank and the Gaza Strip as 'Occupied Territories'. The state of Israel had been created to a large extent by Jews who had escaped from appalling injustice and wicked persecution, from the anti-semitism of Nazi Germany, from the Soviet Union and from countries around the world where Jews had suffered; their longing for some sort of security for themselves in Israel may be claimed as an excuse for their denials of the rights of others under their rule. As a result of Jewish immigration and conquest, there were more than two million Palestinian refugees registered with the United Nations Relief and Works Agency in 1987. Here I propose to deal only with those injustices which Palestinians have suffered in the Occupied Territories of the West Bank and the Gaza Strip.

There are many Israelis and Jews inside and outside Palestine who deplore the treatment of the Palestinians in the Occupied Territories by the Israelis. They are people with uneasy consciences and with minds which are clarifying now. At the time of writing, women in black gather on Fridays on a traffic island in King George Street in the centre of Jerusalem. They carry placards saying in Hebrew, 'Down with the occupation'; and they invite motorists to hoot twice if they agree with them. In *The Observer* of 7 February 1988, Abba Eban, formerly Foreign Minister of Israel, argued:

Two days ago, Israel's leading academic figures, including those who never before uttered a controversial political word, joined together in their hundreds, to urge an early end to the occupation régime ... I came away from my last visit to Gaza with the feeling that it would take a Dante to give adequate literary expression to the intensive concentration of dejection, bitterness and despair crowded into a small, squalid enclave of gloom. It must have been a long time since anyone last smiled in Gaza ... Extremism in Gaza is a reason for ending the occupation, not an excuse of (*sic*) perpetuating it.

To this the Right Hon. Sir Ian Gilmour replied:

The Israeli Government of which Mr Eban was Foreign Minister began the illegal practice of creating 'settlements' on the West Bank and Gaza – a euphemism for pinching land, removing its Palestinian inhabitants, and handing it over to Jews recently arrived from other countries. As a result, more than half of the West Bank has been appropriated and is in the hands of some 60,000 Israelis, while over 800,000 Palestinians have to make do with the rest. And in Gaza, one of the most densely populated areas in the world, more than 40% of the land has been taken by Israel.[4]

There would indeed be difficulties in withdrawing from the Occupied Territories. Since the occupation in 1967, 52% of the West Bank has been confiscated by the Israeli authorities for immediate or future use of Israeli settlers. Over a hundred and twenty Israeli settlements have already been established in the Occupied Territories. This is in clear contradiction of the international law which forbids an occupying power to import its citizens and plant them in an occupied area. Less than half of the country has to support 800,000 Palestinians living in 400 villages and towns. In the Gaza Strip, an Israeli agency reported in 1988 that the density of population was 'amongst the highest in the world', there being between 2,100 and 2,200 people per square kilometre.[5] The Israeli Government has declared more than one-third of the Strip to be 'state land' for Jewish colonization.[6] The Strip, an area of 2,270 square miles, was the home of 65,000 Palestinians at the time of the Six Day War of 1967.[7]

Hundreds of thousands of Palestinian refugees, mostly small landowners, farm workers and labourers, lost their homes when they fled from the advancing Israelis in the 1948 War. Many of them found refuge in the Gaza Strip and the West Bank. British television viewers have had glimpses on their screens of the appalling conditions in the refugee camps. There are serious problems of inadequate housing, inadequate sewerage, inadequate medical services in the West Bank and the Gaza Strip. Twelve out of the fifteen 'population units' (cities, villages and camps) in the Gaza Strip were described in the 1988 *Report* as having 'no sewerage systems, resulting in cholera' and as having an infant mortality rate 'four times the level in Israel'. The Palestinians who live in the Occupied Territories find it hard to secure jobs there. 30% of West Bank workers and nearly 50% of Gaza Strip workers are employed in the Israeli economy, working in construction, cleaning, gardening and dishwashing, and 14% in agriculture.

Those of us who have been to Palestine find the attitude of many of the young, seemingly ill-trained, Israeli soldiers aggressive. A British resident of the West Bank in 1988 described the manner of some of them as 'arrogant and very provocative'. In the Occupied Territories, they carry their rifles in such a way that they are obviously ready to use them quickly. An Oxford graduate, just back at the time of writing, says that she was 'shocked' and 'frightened' when she met these young soldiers policing the streets of a West Bank town. They have powers of arrest for 'security offences' (or suspected security offences). A 1987 press release from the Arab-British Centre declares:

It is estimated that during the 20 years of occupation half a million Palestinians have been arrested or detained for 'security reasons'.

At the moment there are about 4,500 political detainees. Of these 3,500 have been tried and sentenced and 1,000 are in detention for interrogation, awaiting trial or 'administratively detained . . .'

Administrative detention was used widely during the early years of the occupation; for example, in 1970 there were 1,131 administrative detainees. However, international pressure meant that it was used less frequently in the late 1970s and early 1980s.

Administrative detention was reintroduced in August 1985 under the 'Iron Fist' policy and between August 1985 and December 1986 261 people were administratively detained. Amnesty International estimates that there are currently 70 administrative detainees.

An administrative detention order can be renewed *ad infinitum*. For example, Ali Awwad al-Jammal spent six years and nine months under administrative detention before his release in March 1982. Upon his release he was promply placed under 'town arrest'.

Town arrest confines the person to their home town or village during the day and their home by night. It can cost those affected their jobs. Access to medical treatment and the fulfilment of basic social obligations can become impossible.

As with administrative detention, the restricted person is not charged with any crime. In 1986 alone there were 67 Palestinians under town arrest.[8]

Human Rights Violations in the West Bank is a publication which consists of affidavits collected in 1983 by the Commission of the Churches on International Affairs. One affidavit refers to the co-operation of an Israeli official named 'Eli' with Israeli soldiers dealing with a Palestinian farmer:

Later on some soldiers came with the Director of Absentee Property, who told me verbally that 45 dunams of my land, next to the 25 dunams in question, had not been tilled or used since 1967 and were therefore government property. I was appalled at this, since I had been tilling and planting this piece of land every year. Eli then came and chased me off my land. I went to my lawyer and told him what had happened and that the 45 dunams had been surveyed by these people and an aerial picture of it had been taken. The lawyer advised me not to accept the picture of my land or sign it and when Eli and some soldiers came to me for that reason, I took the picture but refused to sign it. I gave the picture to the lawyer and he then put in a request to the High Court to allow me to work on my land, excluding the 25 dunams. The court gave me permission. Eli came to me with a legal adviser and told me that I could work on the 45 dunams pending the final verdict of the High Court. This was on 27 September 1981.

I started to plant my land with grape vines, but was surprised when three soldiers and three others came. One of them ordered me off my land, saying that it belonged to his father. When I refused to leave, he kicked me and two others started beating my son Mahmoud, who was helping me that day. I was trying to defend my son when one of them started shooting in the air. We were adamant and stayed on our land until one of the settlers asked the six offenders to leave us, which they finally did. My children later found two of the bullets. After this incident I went to see my lawyer and during my absence an Israeli came to my house claiming to be the assistant of the Military Governor and took two of my children to the Ramallah military headquarters. They were held there for a while, before being allowed home. Meanwhile, on the advice of my lawyer, I had obtained two medical reports, one stating that I had suffered concussion, the other stating that my son's spinal cord had been injured. I took the reports to the police who informed me that the settlers were bringing a case against me for fighting them. 'But', I said, 'they were seven and I was one, and they were the ones who came to me.'

On 2 November 1981, as my son was tilling the 45 dunams, an Israeli officer, by the name of Yousef, came to him and hit him in the face. My son ran away, but the officer chased him. At this point I came out of the house, and the officer ordered me to go with him to the military headquarters in Ramallah, which I did. I stayed there until twelve noon when the officer returned and, after confiscating my identity card and telling me that I must return the next day at 8.00 am, sent me home. The next day I reported as required, but had to wait until noon before the officer appeared and gave me back my identity card and apologized for not knowing that there was already a case between me and the Military Government regarding my land. I told him there were several cases, but, of course, how is an officer like him to know about such cases. He does not own land that the settlers are trying to grab; land is not his main source of livelihood as it is for me and my family.

Many in the Occupied Territories find themselves in detention pending their trials. *Al-Haq*, the West Bank affiliate of the International Commission of Jurists, describes a detention centre named Dahriyyeh, opened since the uprising of 1987–8:

On 1 May 1988, around 650 detainees were being held at Dahriyyeh. The number of those admitted to the centre since its establishment, however, exceeds 3,000.

Arbitrariness in applying punitive measures, whether provided for by law, like arrest, or illegal, like beating, is a common element in the Israeli response to the Palestinian uprising.

The Israeli military orders grant wide powers of arrest to

soldiers. According to Military Order 378, every soldier is entitled to arrest any person for 18 days without a court order, on the basis of *suspicion* that he committed a 'security offence'. There is no provision to say that this suspicion must be a reasonable one. Every Palestinian is therefore at risk of arrest and detention for up to 18 days, which does not have to be justified before any legal authority.

New rules concerning administrative detention and the inherent bias of the military courts in the Occupied Territories towards believing the Israeli soldiers' testimony further encourage arbitrariness ...

Members of all sectors of Palestinian society are being held in Dahriyyeh: journalists, students, merchants, university lecturers, intellectuals, workers, farmers, blind, crippled, deaf and mute people, and even the mentally retarded ... men as young as 15 and as old as 70. The centre even holds some who were injured by the Israeli army and are still in need of medical care.

Every detainee who has passed through Dahriyyeh, ragardless of his physical condition, his age, his professional and social status, has gone through a process of intimidation at the hands of the Israeli soldiers ...

All the reports gathered by Al-Haq on Dahriyyeh Detention Centre confirm that the process of beating and humiliation starts from the moment the detainees are collected for transport to the centre.

Blindfolded and handcuffed, their hands behind their backs, detainees are pushed by soldiers to a bus to be taken to Dahriyyeh. The bus makes several stops at military government buildings in the West Bank to collect more detainees. Each detainee has to sit with his head bowed below the level of the seat back and is ordered not to make any move. On the way to Dahriyyeh, soldiers beat, shout at and insult the detainees and hit their clubs against the seats, creating an atmosphere of terror.

Another Oxford graduate has spent two years in the Occupied Territories doing social work with young Palestinians. He has a mature and balanced mind. He wrote in the spring of 1988:

The boys came back as we expected on the 1st of February but they were with us for only three days when all the schools in the Occupied Territories were closed down by military order 'until further notice'. So the boys went home again, and all educational institutions have remained closed since the 3rd of February. The reason for the closure was that 'students were gathering in the schools to organize demonstrations'. This is true in some circumstances but with an elementary school like our own it is hardly applicable. The closure of schools adds to the frustration and hopelessness felt by so many Palestinians and does nothing to alleviate the tension of occupation. It is quite possible that the schools will not re-open this academic year.

The three days that the boys were back were action-packed in many ways. On their first day here, one of the Home's two cars was completely destroyed in an arson attack from unidentified sources. It was a pretty frightening experience.

The uprising continues with vigour and the unanimous support of all Palestinians and shows no sign of fading away. The gatherings for worship have become a focus for demonstrations after prayers at the mosques on Fridays, and after church services on Sundays. People go from the house of God to the violence of street confrontation because this is the only form of expression left open to them. There are invariably brutal beatings and killings as a result of such confrontations. Morning worship at the Anglican church is often disrupted by women and children fleeing from tear-gas and pursuing soldiers. Such incidents are accepted with a quiet resignation but there is no doubt that the bitterness builds up under the surface. The Israeli government has tried to suggest that the uprising is largely the result of agitation by Islamic fundamentalists. This is nothing short of a fallacy: the strength of the uprising is that it has the active support of all Palestinians – Moslem, Christian and non-believers alike ...

The situation in the refugee camps continues to be severe. Jalazone and Amari ... have had complete curfews lasting for over two weeks. Many people have come to our Home, having 'escaped' from their refugee camp, asking for food or clothes. Fuad, a friend of mine from the Jalazone camp, was dragged out of bed last Saturday morning to be arrested along with 60 others. His family have no idea where he is.

Just this morning we were witness to an example of unnecessary aggression on the part of the army. After church, the congregations of the Anglican and Roman Catholic churches joined on a peaceful march into the centre of the town. It was a general protest against the occupation, but it was provoked specifically by the assault yesterday on the Roman Catholic priest by Israeli soldiers. After we had walked a short distance, we were confronted by soldiers who fired tear-gas into the centre of our crowd without any provocation. Panic ensued, stone-throwing youths appeared on the scene, and the march became a shambles ...

It is the very fact of the occupation which is most offensive to Palestinians. Now in its 21st year, the illegal occupation of Arab lands has meant a denial of basic human rights and a frustration of the social and cultural life of Palestine. The frustration of anybody who is forced to live in this situation is quite natural; and what we have seen over the last month has been a civil uprising which has been totally spontaneous in its origin, and very widespread in its support. The Israeli government has alleged that the unrest has been orchestrated by PLO extremists; yet what is unique about the latest unrest is that it has brought together all Palestinians, without outside directives, in their quest for basic human rights, including self-determination.

The Palestinians want no more than the right to determine their own future. Forty years after they lost most of their land to the newly formed State of Israel, and twenty years after they were illegally occupied by Israel, self-determination is still denied them. Little wonder that their frustration develops into anger and their anger boils over into violence.

The Palestinians want peace with justice, and the Israeli government is the only body that can give them that justice. Yet far from justice, the government gives them bullets and curfews and deports their political leaders. Nearly forty people have died in the present unrest.

He is emphatic that all who live where he now works are new to the town since the War of 1948. The camps around the town are composed of refugees from 1948 and their descendants. He writes of the 'steady development of hatred' for the Israelis among the Palestinians. All seem to be involved in this hatred; all have developed a political consciousness. There has been appalling provocation. It is known that the United Nations and the European Economic Community have protested concerning Israeli policy in the Occupied Territories. No international pressure seems to secure reduction of Israeli pressure on the peoples of the Occupied Territories. They see no hope from any pressure from outside. They find themselves driven to action from within if there is to remain any chance of shifting the Israelis, of removing Israeli injustice from their land.

An Amnesty International Report of June 1988 declares that 'Amnesty International is concerned because tear-gas has been deliberately misused by Israeli Defence Force persons in the Occupied Territories' during the first five months of the year. It has been used in high concentrations of population in residential areas where it is difficult for the old, the sick and babies to escape quickly. Tear-gas containers appear to have been thrown or fixed into people's homes, health clinics, schools and mosques. In one instance an individual was deliberately shut in a room which was then sprayed with tear-gas. Local medical personnel reported that within a few months more than forty Palestinians in the Occupied Territories had died as a result of the use of tear-gas.[9] A month later, in the course of Palestinian demonstrations, marches and stone-throwing, it was reckoned that 'Israelis are shooting dead Palestinians at the rate of about one every three days.'[10] The same account declares that a thirteen-year-old Palestinian boy had been shot in Gaza in the previous week. A twelve-year-old boy was killed in the previous February; and television gave us some pictures of the brutal beating for forty minutes of two young Palestinians by four Israeli soldiers. Rocks were used with which to break their arms. 'Cruel soldiers are bad soldiers,' Neal Ascherson has declared. Television cameras have recorded for us the bulldozing into rubble of the houses of offending Palestinians. Thousands of houses have been demolished or 'sealed' in the Occupied Territories where Military Commanders have suspected 'connections' with the committing of offences.[11] These tragic attacks which add to the housing shortage have been committed on houses inhabited by large families perhaps only remotely related to the alleged offender. They have taken place before the offender was tried. Sir Ian Gilmour calls Palestine 'a land of the disinherited'.[12]

Fr Gabriel Sinden, of the Society of the Sacred Mission, my old friend from Adelaide, wrote from Jerusalem in mid-1988:

The Palestinian uprising, which began in mid-December, has had a transforming effect on the Palestinians who still live in their homeland – in Israel proper and in the Administered Territories (Gaza and the West Bank of Judea and Samaria). The uprising was triggered off by the prospect of Israel's celebration of forty years of independent statehood in 1988 and the fact that 1987 marked the twentieth anniversary of the Israeli occupation of the Territories in 1967 – which simply took over from the previous nineteen years of Jordanian occupation. The uprising was entirely spontaneous when it broke out in mid-December and has continued to be so ...

It would be quite false to represent the uprising as simply passive resistance. Stones and rocks – and Molotov cocktails – *are* weapons, and no Israeli soldiers or civilians have been killed by them, despite the very real dangers of their being seriously injured by these primitive weapons. It is an ironic version of David and Goliath all over again, and little David still uses only a sling and stone ... The Goliath Israeli response of real bullets, rubber bullets, billy clubs, tear-gas and mace has resulted in hundreds of Palestinians wounded and more than 80 (some Palestinian sources say more than 100) killed since mid-December ...

By the uprising the Palestinians have served notice that they want to live *with* the Israelis and not *under* them. By the same token, Israel must eventually come to terms with this reality, which means, for them, sitting down at a conference table (I would think they would be better protected if this were under International/United Nations auspices) with the PLO. The unsavoury reputation of the PLO is partly deserved, by some sections, no doubt, but it remains the only broadly-based and duly elected body the Palestinians have to represent them. And it is my firm belief that when this happens, it will be for the good of the Israelis as well as for the good of the Palestinians.

The effect of the uprising on those most directly involved is very different. For the first time in forty years the Palestinians are standing tall. They are still a suf ering

people, but they are not bowed down by their suffering. They have found a new courage, a new dignity, and a new sense of identity even when dignity and identity seem to be denied to them by their political situation. With noticeable discipline and very restricted use of force, they have discovered that they are not powerless and they are literally 'irrepressible'. They know themselves to be people to be reckoned with.

American protection saves Israel from suffering under international pressure. So it seems that we who enjoy justice and freedom are prohibited from attempting to help the Palestinians of the Occupied Territories. Christians, however, cannot, must not, be neutral in mind when a people suffers injustice.

We have to consider how we can help, with prayer certainly, and surely by other means. Those who are fighting or who are prepared to fight in the Occupied Territories for an end to Israeli rule, for a more just society, need support financially for a campaign which incites to violence. Without violence there is no prospect whatsoever of an ending to the present Israeli unjust rule. The active unrest in 1988 in the Occupied Territories has already begun to achieve results. We have read what Mr Eban, the former Foreign Minister, has had to say. More recently in August 1988, the Prime Minister of Israel, Mr Yitzhak Shamir, has surprised his hearers and readers. He says: 'The permanent status of these territories is a separate subject for negotiations. We are ready to negotiate with the Palestinians, we are ready to negotiate with Egypt, we are ready to negotiate with Jordan.'[13] As a self-admitted former terrorist, he knows that violence works, admits implicitly that it is working with Israel. 'Our concept is that

Arabs and Jews have to live together here, we cannot change it,' he adds. The unbending and powerful Israelis are beginning to consider yielding in some measure to the force of an outraged people. There is nothing other than force which would cause them to consider yielding. The Palestinian violence which is a desperate cry for an end to injustice deserves support.

I was brought up in a part of Kentucky where we tended to look down on 'the Negro'. I have never quite lost that racial prejudice acquired in childhood. Nevertheless, South Africa shook and disturbed me when I first saw the narrow telephone kiosks for blacks and the wide ones for whites, when I discovered the separate public lavatories for each race, and when I found that I could not go into the same public bar with my black friend. All this was in the days before the official policy of apartheid. Bishop John Taylor recalls his sense of shame and pain when he found that whites and blacks used different entrances to the same railway station. These surely were intuitive human reactions to inhuman divisions within society. In South Africa in the late 1980s young men about to be called up for the armed forces are expressing doubts as to whether they ought to serve in a system where they may be required to enforce inter-racial distinctions. Etienne Marais, president of the Students' Representative Council at the University of Witwatersrand, declared that when he served in the Defence Force infantry in 1980–81, he found himself involved in the shooting of a 30-year-old woman, the torture of a 16-year-old girl, and the firing of rifle grenades into villages before they had been checked for civilian inhabitants.[14] A group of fresh-faced young South African whites has been seen on British television, all agreed that they have no intention of serving in a Defence Force liable to engage in such anti-black cruelty. There have been young men before in South Africa who have protested against conscription and who have been to prison for doing so. For them there was not the international publicity which has been generated in 1988.

Apartheid was 'the central theme of the era that began in 1948' in South Africa.[15] Behind it lay the Calvinist doctrine of the Afrikaaners that God has ordered life as it is in South Africa in accordance with his revealed will. Dr H. Verwoerd explained implications of the doctrine of apartheid in 1954: 'It comprises the political sphere; it is necessary in the social sphere; it is aimed at in church matters; it is relevant to every sphere of life.'[16] Dr Verwoerd became Prime Minister in 1958. He had a clear and vigorous mind. He made himself more explicit:

> South Africa is a white man's country and ... he must remain the master here. In the reserves we are prepared to allow the Native to be the masters; we are not the masters there. But within the European areas, we, the white people of South Africa, are and shall remain the masters.[17]

Dr Verwoerd was stabbed to death on 6 September 1966. He was a man idolized by many.

The claim of the supporters of apartheid is that whites are responsible for making the civilized, prosperous South Africa of today, with its developed agriculture, industry and commerce. They have earned their right to control primarily for their own benefit the bulk of the territory of the Republic. For the blacks there are the 'bantustans', the 'Homelands', eight areas designed to become autonomous states for the blacks. Some of these areas are not intact pieces of land, but are 'scattered little bits of the most unyielding soil' (Steve Biko). In the midst of each are the productive areas reserved for white farmers of the Republic. None has access to a major port, and mineral rights in all are reserved for the Republic. For the blacks based in the Republic, political rights are few. 'We are at the mercy of them,' says a bright but sad young black politician on British television. A South African Cabinet Minister, speaking on the radio to Britain, declares that whites do not claim to have better brains than blacks, but do need an environment in which they can be themselves. Whites and blacks, say the exponents of apartheid, need 'separate development'. A massive report of a Commission in 1956 took the view that there was 'little hope of evolutionary development towards a common society for whites and blacks', 'not the slightest ground for believing that the European population, either now or in the future, would be willing to sacrifice its character as a national entity and as a European racial group'.[18]

Let us consider how the policy of white superiority within the Republic works out. It is commonly believed that there are 26 million blacks in South Africa. In 1988, the South African Government claims that the latest figures available (those of 1985) show that the whites comprise 17.8% of the population of the Republic. The Government says that the blacks comprise 68.8%, the coloureds (of mixed race) 10.3%, the Indians 3.1%. It excludes from the black population over 2 million blacks based on the so-called independent states of Transkei, Cisbei, Bophuthatswana and Venda. These figures speak for themselves. The large black majority, in fact perhaps 85%, owns only 13% of the land and earns on the average only a quarter of what whites earn. There is a doctor for every 400 whites and one for every 4,000 blacks; more than three times as much is spent on a white child's education as on a black child's. Many skilled jobs and apprenticeships are reserved for whites. All blacks must carry 'reference books' containing their photographs and their records. The Republic is indeed a white man's land. Blacks have no votes for the parliament of the Republic. Behind all this, there is an unavowed contempt for the capacity of the black. As an educated and utterly charming South African lady of English extraction once said to me in Durban: 'You simply cannot trust the natives; I have had fifteen or sixteen servants, and you could not trust one of them.' To do him justice, her husband protested.

Since the 'state of emergency' was declared in June 1986, about 30,000 blacks have been arrested. Amongst these have been perhaps as many as 10,000 children under the age of sixteen. A recent Amnesty International report declared that children as young as seven years old had been taken into custody. 'Most of them', says the report, 'have been assaulted. Some of them were beaten, whipped and kicked for several hours, and others given electric shocks.' This is the kind of 'official action' which is sometimes authorized, sometimes 'just happens'. It is all indicative of the attitude of many whites. So too are such 'unofficial actions', as that taken in the case of Eric Sambo. He drove into and killed accidentally two of his employer's son's dogs. He was tied to a tree, punched and sjambokked for two days, and died after the second night. This was in December 1987.

The Guardian of 24 August 1988 reports: Joseph X, a 30-year-old black South African, was in detention for four months. Kept in solitary confinement he was beaten up, regularly interrogated, and had electric shocks to his testicles. Released without ever being charged, he had lost his job, suffered from sexual problems and had difficulty in sleeping. His concentration was poor and he had become remote from other people. Raymond Suttner was a senior lecturer in the University of the Witwatersrand. He is a white man. He was arrested in 1986, and spent more than two years in prison, without being tried, or even charged. He was kept in solitary confinement. When he was released in 1988, he was banned from any educational or public involvement. Such is the injustice, the measure of imposed human suffering.

The African National Congress was formed on 8 January 1912. For decades it sought reform by peaceful methods, striving for full and equal rights for blacks in the land of their

birth. In its Freedom Charter of 26 June 1955, it declared that
'South Africa belongs to all who live in it, black and white
...', that 'our people have been robbed of their birthright,
their land, liberty and peace, by a form of government
founded on injustice and inequality'. It asked for 'peace and
friendship among all our people, to be secured by upholding
the equal rights, opportunities and status of all'. In 1961, it
embarked on the road of armed struggle, claiming that every
other route to justice and freedom had been closed. Nelson
Mandela, its brilliant and highly respected leader, was
arrested on 5 August 1962 and tried, with others arrested at
Rivonia, near Johannesburg, in the famous 'Rivonia case'. He
was sentenced to life imprisonment on 12 June 1964. He is the
winner of the Simon Bolivar Prize for Liberation, of India's
Jawaharlal Nehru award for International Understanding, of
the Commonwealth Secretariat's Third World Prize, and of
other international honours. He is an honorary citizen of
Rome and of Glasgow, of Florence and of Aberdeen. He
declared in the course of his four and a half hour speech in his
own defence at the trial:

> I have cherished the ideal of a democratic and free society
> in which all persons live together in harmony and with
> equal opportunities. It is an ideal which I hope to live for
> and to achieve. But if needs be, it is an ideal for which I am
> prepared to die.

Earlier in his speech he had said:

> The hard facts were that fifty years of non-violence had
> brought the African people nothing but more and more
> repressive legislation and fewer and fewer rights. It may not
> be easy for this court to understand, but it is a fact that for
> a long time the people had been talking of violence ... and
> we, the leaders of the ANC, had always prevailed upon

them to avoid violence and to pursue peaceful methods. . .
At the beginning of June 1961, after a long and anxious
assessment of the South African situation, I and some
colleagues came to the conclusion that, as violence in this
country was inevitable, it would be unrealistic and wrong
for African leaders to continue preaching peace and non-
violence at a time when the Government met our peaceful
demands with force.

Mr Mandela is a Christian and a student of the Bible;[19] the
ANC has become 'almost a folk organization in South Africa'
(according to Reginald September). 'It is here,' said an old
woman, touching her breast. Then she opened her arms, as if
to embrace the whole room, and added, 'It is here.'[20]

If Mr Mandela is a sick but living martyr, Steve Biko,
a younger man, battered towards his death by the South
African police in 1977, made an impact not only for 'Black
Consciousness' on young black students in the South African
universities, but upon all those of all races who have seen the
celebrated film *Cry Freedom* made in 1986–7 to portray him.
He was a baptized and confirmed member of the Anglican
Church. However, he became adversely critical of a white-
dominated church and, indeed, of Christianity itself as he
found it in South Africa. It seemed to him to have become a
white phenomenon. He himself made a significant contribution towards an emerging 'black theology'. Fr Aelred Stubbs
of the Community of the Resurrection, Mirfield, describes
him as 'one who, had he lived, might well have been the first
Prime Minister of a united, non-racial, democratic South
Africa'. Of the whites Steve Biko wrote in 1971:

My promise has always been that black people should not
at any one stage be surprised at some of the atrocities
committed by the government. This to me follows logically
after their initial assumption that they, being a settler

minority, can have the right to be supreme masters. If they could be cruel enough to cow the natives down with brutal force and install themselves as perpetual rulers in a foreign land, then anything else they do to the same black people becomes logical in terms of the initial cruelty.

That is the black point of view, strange indeed to us colonizers. He goes on:

To expect justice from them at any stage is to be naïve ... The absolutely infantile evidence upon which the State builds up its cases in some of the trials does suggest to me that they are quite capable of arresting a group of boys playing hide-and-seek and charging them with high treason.[21]

Steve Biko was a friendly person, not a bitter man. He had an able brain, a brilliant capacity for self-expression, a great sense of humour. He enabled some whites to begin to understand how blacks felt. Such men as the mature Mandela and the young Biko made impressions on the minds of white people which caused them to realize what the black peoples of South Africa are capable of.

In 1987, a group of 58 South African whites, mostly Afrikaners, including politicians, political scientists and business men, after talks in Senegal with 17 of the ANC leadership, issued a 'Dakar Declaration'. It stated that the group had 'developed an understanding of the conditions which have generated a wide-spread revolt by the black people as well as the importance of the ANC as a factor in resolving the conflict'. Only two of the 58 refused to sign it. The Commonwealth Eminent Persons Group, headed by a former Conservative Prime Minister of Australia, was allowed in 1986 to interview Mr Mandela in prison. After meeting and listening to South African leaders including the President of the Republic, it came to the following conclusion: 'We have examined the government's "programme reform" and have been forced to conclude that at present there is no genuine intention of the South African government to dismantle apartheid.' It recommended economic sanctions, saying that the imposition of these might be 'the last chance to avert what could be the worst bloodbath since the Second World War'. The Group concluded:

> Put in the most simple way, the blacks have had enough of apartheid. They are no longer prepared to submit to its oppression, discrimination and exploitation. They can no longer stomach being treated as aliens in their own country.

There has been a lack of will amongst the greater trading countries to apply the kind of sanctions which will really hurt in South Africa. Blacks there have learnt that from the West will come deep sympathy but little practical support. As Neal Ascherson has said of a different situation: 'Today, we know that we have no guarantees: we are alone.' The Reverend Frank Chikane, General Secretary of the South African Council of Churches, said in London in July 1988: 'We in South Africa have learnt the hard way that the major Western countries will not apply effective sanctions against the apartheid régime unless the voters in those countries take a stand to force their governments to do so.' Voters and governments do little or nothing of the kind. Chikane speaks with experience of suffering, while well-intentioned people look on:

> We are a new generation who are born to pain. Recently in a national conference of the South African Council of Churches, it dawned on me as I looked around that we are almost a generation of prisoners and detainees ... No one can be neutral during a moment of truth. All are political: so are we, on the side of justice.[22]

Dr Allan Boesak, a wise and learned theologian of the black Reformed Church in South Africa, has been described as 'the pulse ... of South Africa's suffering black people'.[23] It was he, more than anybody, who persuaded the General Council of the World Alliance of Reformed Churches at Ottawa in 1982 to declare 'that apartheid is a sin and that the moral and theological justification of it is a travesty of the gospel, a betrayal of the Reformed tradition, and a heresy'. A meeting of world church leaders with trade unionists and others issued in May 1987 a 'Lusaka Document'. This was adopted by the South African Council of Churches in July of the same year. It went much further. It stated that 'the nature of the South African régime ... compels the (opposition) movements to the use of force along with other means to end oppression'. It declared that during the past eleven months, more than 20,000 opponents of apartheid had been detained. Again black children of seven are mentioned as detainees. It affirmed the right of the people of South Africa to secure justice and peace through the liberation movements.

Christians were being driven by continuing injustice to justify force, as they attempted to work out the implications of the earlier and famous 'Kairos Document' of 25 September 1985, drawn up by 150 prominent South African Christians. It described apartheid:

> Apartheid is a system whereby a minority régime elected by one small section of the population is given an explicit mandate to govern in the interests of, and for the benefit of, the white community. Such a mandate is by definition hostile to the common good of all the people. In fact, because it tries to rule in the exclusive interests of whites and not in the interests of all, it ends up by ruling in a way that is not even in the interests of those whites.

The Document challenged:

> The time has come. The moment of truth has arrived.
> South Africa has been plunged into a crisis that is shaking
> the foundations, and there is every indication that the crisis
> has only just begun and that it will deepen and become
> even more threatening in the months to come. It is the
> KAIROS or moment of truth not only for apartheid but also
> for the church.

I propose to use some of the writing of President Kaunda
of Zambia and one of the Resolutions of the Lambeth
Conference to illustrate developments in the thinking of
Christians as they find themselves struggling in their minds
with the continuing injustice of South Africa. President
Kaunda is known to be a gentle, peace-loving Christian. He
had visited India. Gandhi, he said, was his ideal; he described
himself as formerly 'the darling of the pacifist cause'.[24] He
noted that Mr Ian Smith, of Rhodesia, was driven out of
power by force, not shamed into making concessions. He
declared that 'passive resistance may strengthen an oppressive
authority if it diverts the people's righteous anger into easily
controlled channels'.[25] He describes passive resistance as 'a
sport for gentlemen (and ladies) . . . a heroic enterprise for the
ruling classes, but a grievous burden laid on the rest'.[26] He
quotes Douglas Jerrold:

> We love peace, but not peace at any price. There is a peace
> more destructive of the manhood of living man than war is
> destructive of his body. Chains are worse than bayonets.

He goes on to say that the South African white minority will
start to 'lose the war' when 'ordinary white citizens are no
longer able to enjoy their stay in paradise because they have
lost for ever their sense of security'.[27] He asserts that 'the

philosophy of black inferiority is enshrined in South Africa's laws and customs and prevents the black people from being themselves ...' 'There can be', he says, 'no development of personality, no room for either excellence or equality, no better tomorrow ...' He concludes: 'Apartheid's challenge not only to Africa but to all humanity is so absolute that if there is no other way we must face up, as the free world has done before in this century, to a long hard struggle which cannot exclude the use of force.'[28] His pacifism has been battered, indeed broken, by the cruel fact of continuing and seemingly unending injustice in South Africa. 'Violence used in the course of a people's war of liberation', he says, 'is not something romantic – it is a cry of despair from the oppressed who can see no other way out.'[29]

In conclusion, I want to say something about the thought and words of Archbishop Desmond Tutu whom Dr Allan Boesak describes as 'a true South African, a champion of the cause of the poor, the weak, the dispossessed ... the man who earned the love and respect of the world'.[30] In an open letter to Desmond Tutu, published in the *Argus* of 16 September 1981, Allan Boesak writes, referring at first to the South African Government's attitude to him:

> You are now considered an enemy of the state, indeed of South Africa, a dangerous 'subversive' who does not 'deserve' a passport ... It is they who have done so much to help convince generations of Black South Africans that non-violent protest has no chance in South Africa. For years we have petitioned, marched, pleaded, cried, tried to speak to the conscience of the South African government. They have answered with police, with detentions and tear gas, with dogs and guns. And with that infinite contempt of those who have nothing left but the power of the gun ... You have a deep love of your country. But they will never understand that. For them, loving South Africa means

accepting apartheid and white supremacy, humiliation and exploitation. It means to bow your head in submission and say 'Ja baas', even if deep in your heart you despise yourself. They do not understand that loving South Africa means precisely to despise apartheid and all that system has made of all of us, white and Black. It is to fight for a country where we shall no longer be ruled by fear and greed.

Frank Chikane tells of a recent talk with the Archbishop. He was just back from the United States. He said that he was tired of going round the world to tell its peoples of African pain 'until', as he said, 'we look like fools'. He added, 'Why expect sympathy from people who will not do anything to intervene?' He went on, 'Maybe we should redefine our priorities, stay at home and fight the system and, maybe, make sure we change it.'[31] Archbishop Tutu played a prominent part in the deliberations of the Lambeth Conference of Anglican bishops at Canterbury in July and August 1988. He said at that Conference:

The church is not pacifist. Our people have used conventional means, and each time the response has been a violent response. We are not asking you to condone or condemn, but to say to those of our people who have tried everything: 'We understand.'

Jean-Marc Ela wrote as long ago as 1984:

The church cannot stay aloof from the fray, searching for the transcendence of the Spirit. It has to remake contact with the African soil, not only with its religions and cultures, but with the humiliations (suffering the violence of imperialism and power), and with the resistance and its struggles.[32]

We go now, briefly, to a consideration of the attempt by another church, the Roman Catholic Church, to work out a 'liberation theology' for those struggling for freedom and justice in South and Central America. The object of the last section of this chapter is not to make a study of authoritarian government in South and Central America, with all its manifestations of injustice and suppression of freedom. It mentions only a few of the gross injustices which have been committed in that continent and a half of authoritarian régimes. It is to introduce the Roman Catholic concept of liberation theology and to say something concerning the 'base communities' of Christians which have become one of the marks of Roman Catholicism in Latin America. Perhaps the most unjust and cruel of dictatorships was to be found in Nicaragua under the Somoza family:

> There was no liberty. The pressures were terrible. Every member of the Guardia was a law unto himself. They killed, robbed, raped and there was no one to complain to. They were the law and against the law. Anyone who complained would be killed. They stole cattle and sold them to one another ... You just couldn't go up to a military man and address him with a problem. They would be as likely to rob you of what you had in your pocket, and arrest you. And if you spoke about it, they would kill you.[33]

It was a credit to the church that some of its priests were in the forefront of opposition to Somoza rule and that four of them took office in the Sandinista Government which replaced it in November 1979. Dr Christopher Rowland speaks from personal experience of this Government. He assures me that Nicaragua is going to be no second Cuba, that there is no good whatsoever to be said of the America-supported 'Contra' rebels. My friend, Dr Peter West, writes on 8 November 1988 of 'a 7-year-old unjust war ... imposed on the country'.

Nicaragua under the Somoza family was poverty-stricken and sparsely populated. Even today each square kilometre only supports eighteen people. With all its present weakness and difficulties it is at least no longer an uncaring régime. Amnesty International in 1988 gave a briefing concerning the human rights emergency in Colombia. It describes a 'policy of terror' on the part of government agents, with '1000 and more political killings in 1987'. It concludes that 'human rights violations on a massive scale' are 'the result of a deliberate policy of political murder'. 'Amnesty has overwhelming evidence ... that killings attributed to the "death squads" are frequently carried out by military and police personnel.' 'Anyone involved in community is at risk,' said a young Colombian in 1986. The level of official violence against civilians has escalated dramatically. There are terrible acts of torture and mutilation of corpses by the death squads. There are brave demonstrations and protests; but the cruelty and the killings go on. By the end of November 1988 there had been twenty mass killings in Colombia during the year. In the course of them 215 people had died.[34] The second city of Colombia is, ironically, Medellín, the city of liberation theology. Dr Sheila Cassidy, in a BBC radio programme on 29 March 1987, described Chile from her terrible personal experience as 'living in a state of violence'. In a BBC television programme on 21 August 1988, it was stated that when General Pinochet became unelected President of Chile in 1973 'justice became deaf and blind'. The church in Chile became united in a political anti-Government outlook. 'Christians can and must be revolutionaries,' proclaimed to us on television one of its leaders. The people of the small, land-locked Republic of El Salvador suffered much violence from its masters. Archbishop Oscar Ranulfo Romero, when he became primate of El Salvador in February 1977, was a basically conservative bishop. He was, however, well aware that the Republic was, in fact, manipulated for their own benefit by the celebrated 'fourteen families'. Their names are Llach, De Sola, Hill, Duenas, Regalado, Wright, Salverria, Garcia Prieto, Quiñones, Guirola, Borja, Sol, Dalio, Meza Ayau. There were (and are) other over-rich families, some better, some worse, many completely lacking in social consciousness. The Archbishop knew the opulence in which they lived, and came to know the gross poverty of the people. At Jicarón, north of San Salvador, in June 1977, he was hungry after a two hour Mass and a long journey by car and on foot. He asked for a little food; there was none to give him; no one had anything to eat in that place that day. The soldiers had ransacked the people's houses, killed their pigs and chickens, scattered their grain.[35] Young devoted priests and others in the base communities in his diocese educated the Archbishop. He saw, he listened, he came to understand. When it seemed that he had come to understand fully, he was shot in the head and instantaneously killed, immediately after saying the words of institution during the consecration in the course of an evening Mass at 6.30 on 24 March 1980. So the death squads continue to act, bitter civil war goes on.

His bishops in El Salvador were hostile to this good man; only one of his own bishops attended his funeral. He himself had learned much from liberation theology. At the Second General Conference of Latin American bishops at Medellín in Colombia in 1968, bishops seemed to take courage from one another. They began to help to develop 'a new theological-pastoral framework ("liberation theology") and a new pastoral methodology (evangelization in lay-led *comunidades de base*)'.[36] Medellín spoke of a 'poor and exploited people ... who are systematically and legally despoiled of their being human'. It claimed that 'sin demands a radical liberation, which necessarily includes liberation of a political nature'. It spoke of 'a sinful situation' and of 'institutionalized violence', and summoned the church 'to establish solidarity with the poor and lowly and to work for their liberation from the social sinfulness that now oppresses them'. Liberation theology may have originated from an essay by Roger Shaull, an American. It certainly went on growing out of the experience of the people. It was not primarily a theology given to them from above, but rather a way for them of 'doing' theology, arising out of the people's need and the people's groping, an emerging theology. Medellín was the bishops' answer to the cry of the people, but it was not accepted whole-heartedly by all the bishops. Liberation theology, with or without the bishops, appealed to the Old Testament struggles of the Israelites to achieve by armed force the freedom which they needed from unjust foreign domination both in Egypt and within Palestine. The Christian neglects the Old Testament and its insights at the peril of his freedom. My admired friend, Dr Peter Hinchliff, of Balliol College, writes that 'the liberation theology of Latin America ... asserts the primacy of a single biblical theme, the liberation of the oppressed, as the basis of all hermeneutics; the Marxian analysis of history and society which makes a contextual morality possible; and the importance of the base community, the group of Christians engaged in political action, as the place where the actual Church is most authoritatively to be found'. He refers to 'the insistence of the liberation theologians that the theology is something *done*, the consequence of *praxis*'.[37] The Institute for Contextual Theology of Johannesburg declared in 1985 that liberation theology was worked out in the context of the 'experience of poverty, powerlessness and domination, of being totally dependent culturally, economically, politically and psychologically, upon the so-called developed nations of North America and Europe and the experience of struggling for liberation from this dependence'.

In his illuminating *Radical Christianity*, Christopher Rowland describes liberation theology as 'the most influential and challenging theological movement in our contempory world'. He considers it to be a continuation of the thread of hope and radical change which has run throughout the fabric of Christian theology. 'The theology of liberation', he writes, 'is the product of a subtle mix of tradition and experience of poverty and oppression for the majority which has enabled the riches of the Christian tradition to be looked at afresh and some of its contents uncovered.' He tells us that this theology emerges from experience of oppression and injustice, but that it develops amidst Bible study by small groups for whom life is interpreted 'with the help of the Bible'.[38] He tells me of base groups of as many as fifty or even a hundred whose meetings he has attended in Brazil. In shanty towns, he says, there may be many base groups meeting weekly.

So liberation theology continues to be discussed, its basic principles taken from the Old Testament and the Gospels. 'For the prophets', the demand for 'mercy and not sacrifice' was 'inseparable from the denunciation of social injustice and from the vigorous assertion that God is known only by doing justice'. The kingdom of God, asserts Gutierrez, is to be 'a Kingdom of contradiction to the established powers and on behalf of humankind'.[39] He claims that the church's duty is to denounce all that is contrary in society to brotherhood, justice, liberty. It is understood that there is a 'school of torture' in operation in Central America (BBC, 4 November 1988). Liberation theology asserts, says Gutierrez, that 'the truth of the Gospel ... is a truth which must be done', that 'the class struggle is a fact that Christians cannot dodge'.[40] Israel had to be freed from slavery in Egypt, and the peoples of Latin America not only from oppression but from poverty. 'In the Bible poverty is a scandalous condition inimical to human dignity and therefore contrary to the will of God', he writes. Material poverty is 'a subhuman situation' to be remedied.[41] Christian love demands such a remedying.

What is especially remarkable about the Latin American base communities is the sense among the Christian poor within them that they must be prepared as God's own people to act on their own. Their own priest may or may not be available to them; but they have their lay leaders, their catechists, 'responsible individuals dedicated to the internal development of the human person and to the formation of communities'.[42] There came with the base communities 'a new pastoralism', a recognition of the active participation of lay people in the work of the church. In El Salvador the base communities consist of about thirty people, with their own elected leaders, catechists or lay teachers. Fifteen hundred leaders were trained there over a recent ten-year period. 'The catechist', said a Salvadorean priest, 'is a man who works not only as a religious person, but assumes leadership that is also social ... at times political in our rural communities.' The leaders draw from the Bibles, distributed wherever possible to community members, the message 'that the poor had the right to seek justice here and now through their own organizations'. One of the Salvadorean base communities' members wrote: 'The priests preached the gospel, but it was us, the peasants, who set up our organization.' Among protestants, who had outgrown their American Evangelical founders and who had pastors of local birth and upbringing, there was a tendency and ability to develop social teaching and thinking akin to that of the base communities. This was especially important in Nicaragua, where the episcopate tended to be unsympathetic to the thinking of the socialistically-inclined base communities. In Nicaragua, and indeed in Brazil, there is a fragility about the base communities because of episcopal disfavour.

Many of the bishops of Latin America came indeed to withdraw support from the liberation theology which they themselves had witnessed to at Medellín. Some of them had been hostile to Medellín from the start. The work of spreading the theology and in varying degrees the action which was called for has been carried on by the base communities. In Chile and Brazil these have spurred religious revivals; in Nicaragua and El Salvador they have been closely associated with revolutionary movements. In Chile from 1969 onwards they have consisted of between 20 and 50 Christians, studying, praying, having dialogue with one another, deciding on the practical implications of a Bible-based Catholic faith. They have their lay co-ordinators; and priests attend them when they can. Archbishop Romero in El Salvador appealed to them: 'Christians who belong to ecclesial base communities ... the Church challenges you to reach out to a goal that will be politically valid. Christians, in this difficult hour, our country needs liberators who are morally good and a liberation that is socially authentic.'[43] During his primacy he learned much from liberation theology and from the base communities themselves. In an interview with *Prensa Latina* on 15 February 1980, he said:

> I believe in the need for the Salvadorean people to become organized ... The organizations are the social force that will promote, and pursue, and be able to create an authentic society ... Organization is necessary to be able to struggle effectively.[44]

Paulo Freire says that where there is oppression, there must be 'critical and liberating dialogue', there must be a 'pedagogical character' in the struggle for freedom, the oppressed must find through that struggle 'their way to life-affirming humanization'.[45] In the base communities, there is sharing of study, there is witnessing to insights, there is sometimes challenge to action. In the course of the development of liberation theology and of the base communities, it sometimes comes to be seen that no distinction can be made between the kinds of social action appropriate to clergy and the kinds appropriate to laity.[46] The obligation on both to love may lead to the duty of political involvement for both. The Jesuit Superiors of Colombia asserted in 1972: 'We feel ourselves as one with the priests, religious and lay people who, following the norms of the hierarchy, and with a truly evangelical spirit, have committed themselves to the defense of the weak and given voice to those who had none.'[47] Giving voice may have to lead on to taking action.

Camilo Torres was a priest, trained in Belgium in sociology, a university chaplain and a community organizer. He 'came to believe that as a Christian he was obliged to be political and to promote revolutionary change'.[48] To be political is indeed in itself no offence against Catholicism; poliitics is concerned with power in community; and the Christian is under no obligation to accept misuse of power as if it were not wrong. However, his belief in the need for revolution resulted in his finding himself conscientiously unable from 1965 to accept ecclesiastical discipline. He was laicized and became leader of a 'United Front' in Colombia. Then he joined guerilla revolutionaries, the 'Army of National Liberation'; he was killed in 1966 in a fight with Chilean government forces. He has been described as one who at all times 'maintained a vital posture of commitment to the people – as a priest, as a Christian, and as a revolutionary'.[49] He died before Medellín, but left his mark on minds. He wrote before he died that he believed that what he was doing was 'the only effective and far-reaching way to make the love of all people a reality'.

It has been said of liberation theology that it 'is ... a developing current with varied directions and emphases'.[50] There are those who remain within the priesthood and within the church who believe that prolonged injustice requires violence if it is to be eliminated. Of M.K. Hellwig's *Jesus – The Compassionate God*, the Bishop of Ely wrote 'the notion of revolt is not far below the surface of this book'.[51] Phillip Berryman, of the American Friends' Service Committee between 1976 and 1980, affirms that there is a Christian case for use of violence: 'It seems to me, in fact, that ... the general legitimacy of the use of violence by opposition groups in Nicaragua, El Salvador and Guatemala must be conceded.'

He explains that this is really grounded in the right of self-defence generally held by Christians to be morally valid (unless, as he says, 'one takes a position of absolute and principled non-violence').[52] I have tried to deal with the non-validity of the pacifist interpretation of the Gospel ethic in the first chapter of this book. A developed liberation theology justifies the Christian in certain circumstances in taking part in revolution. Conscientious English Christians took part with varying degrees of violence in the Great Rebellion and the Glorious Revolution of the seventeenth century. Latin American liberation theology challenges all concerned with the need for revolution against continuing injustice to plan carefully and in detail for the construction of a just social order to take the place of the unjust one to be destroyed. Revolutionaries in Ireland are beginning to think now along these constructive lines. The hierarchy of the church needs to think hard concerning the validity of the action of Christians obliged by moral imperative to help to overthrow an unjust order. This may well involve the taking of life. If the hierarchy can justify the taking of life in war in a just cause, it can do the same in the case of revolution against enduring injustice. Louie G. Hechanova, CSSR, wrote in 1986:

> There is an option that lies between the extremes of pacifism and brutal, terroristic, irresponsible violence. The option is to undertake a revolution for justice's sake, even in the name of Christian love, in which the risks of giving one's life for others could become the highest expression of Christian love. There is, therefore, room for 'responsible violence' which is motivated not by hate but love ... and which is calculated to usher in a new era of justice, truth, freedom, love and peace.[53]

CHAPTER SIX

War

We come now to international war, to the rightness (or wrongness) of sometimes using force between two nations. There were only twenty-one years between the Great War of 1914–18 and the Second World War of 1939–45. More than forty years have passed since that War. During those forty years there have been extreme tensions, a 'cold war', with real fears that all this might lead to a real war between NATO and the Warsaw Pact powers. The fact remains that, despite fear, prejudice, imperialism, there has been no Third World War. There was always a drawing back at the brink.

There can be no doubt that what saved the peace was the possession on both sides of nuclear weapons. No one cares for these, because of their terrifying potential for destruction. However, everyone knows that, whatever ghastly damage the first user of such weapons may inflict, the other side, from land or sea or air, will retaliate with nuclear weapons. Fearful damage may then be done to the side which first used them. No side dares to start. Nuclear weapons have indeed saved the peace for many tense and bitter years, acting as deterrents. It is a shame and mistake to call these nuclear weapons 'evil'. In the modern sense of the word, there is moral connotation. An evil man or woman has made a choice, at least in thought. The nuclear weapon has no choice-making capacity; it is an instrument of the choice-maker. One has no right to cloud the issue by describing it as if it had made a moral decision. It lies inert, neither innocent nor guilty, the tool of bad or good people. At the present time, with the enlightened new thinking of the leaders of the Soviet Union, it seems to be the instrument of good and wise men of both sides, recognized by NATO and the USSR as an accepted means of preserving the peace. Now the Soviet Union which seemed to ex-President Reagan in 1986 to be 'the evil empire', has become a friendly power in which in 1988, he could walk smilingly, shaking hands in the streets of Moscow.

A writer in *The Guardian* in 1987 described 'the bomb' as a peace-preserver:

Once upon a very recent time, Europe was the cockpit of war, perpetually riven by advancing armies, death and devastation. But the 40 years since the bomb have been 40 years of peace. Mankind hasn't stopped making war. To the contrary, nations beyond the nuclear umbrella have been waging it decade after decade. Look today at Iran and Iraq, pouring the blood of children into the sands in a struggle whose toll matches the fields of Flanders. But Europe, meanwhile, even with the fault line of a divided Germany across it, remains stable and prosperous. And the two great nations who, in their disparate ideologies, might go to war – the USA and the USSR – have not done so. The bomb may be a terrible weapon; but because it is so terrible it may be that it cannot be used. A thesis proved every year over 40 years. We throw away that repulsive crutch at our peril.[1]

Now at the end of the 1980s, men and women of the Eastern forces and men and women of the West begin to mingle as friends, thanks to the deterrent capacity of nuclear weapons. These must remain in being so long as inter-Great Power tensions exist. Already the tensions have lessened. When war becomes as impossible between the USA and the USSR as it now is between the United States and Britain, let nuclear arms be scrapped (so long as we are sure no lesser nations have them). In the meantime, as understanding relationships develop between the Western nations and the Soviet Union, the exorbitant number of nuclear weapons on both sides is being (all too slowly) reduced. As I write, I hear on the radio of the wholesale destruction of Soviet SS20 missiles not very far from Moscow in the presence of NATO observers.

It was reckoned early in the 1980s that there had been 127 wars in the world since 1945 (according to the Brookings Institute).[2] One such war, from April to June 1982, was that of Great Britain and Argentina, over the Falkland Islands. Here was a war provoked by an invasion of the British-held and British-inhabited Falklands by a power which had not been connected with these islands for a century and a half. There was a Christian case for the British Government to send a force to rescue the Falkland Islanders from an invasion by the military government of another country. That country made it plain that it had no intention of withdrawing under international or any diplomatic pressure. What Christians cannot be satisfied with was the British Government's refusal to discuss before the Falklands War the whole question of whether it would not be more sensible and economical for the islands to be transferred to nearby Argentina and the British inhabitants to be transferred at government cost to other areas where they might live and work under similar conditions. This would at any rate have been worthy of serious international consideration, as the United Nations urged.

None of us would justify the USSR invasion of Czechoslovakia on 22 August 1968, but some would justify the US invasion of Grenada in October 1983. We Christians ought to be rational and vocal whenever international military action is taken, and especially, if possible, before it is taken, when it is proposed. I am not prepared to outline fully once again the mediaeval 'just war' doctrine which owed much to St Thomas Aquinas, as well as to St Augustine, and even to St Ambrose. Nor am I prepared to appeal to it. It is not that it is invalid, but that it is on the one hand remote in thought and language from the Bible and the Gospel, and on the other hand remote from the conditions of modern warfare. It asks for the exclusion of civilians from direct military action; and we know that modern military action, from the air and from the sea and from long-range weapons, is bound to be injurious on a huge scale to innocent civilians. From a biblical and Christian point of view, we Christians can painfully accept this. We are all bound up together, of one body, having to learn to share with one another in suffering. 'Whether one member suffer, all the members suffer with it' (I Cor. 12.26, AV). The doctrine also demands that we do not go to war unless there is a reasonable chance of winning it. That is sound and good. Those who believe the Soviet system to be misguided, some of its practices inhuman, rightly do not urge us to risk our lives in a vain military effort to overturn it. This wise principle must cause us to look again at the 'wars' being fought by IRA and ANC against strong governments with strong armed forces. Both IRA and ANC wishfully believe that there is hope of winning these 'wars'. Mr Gerry Adams declares that his friends are 'very mindful of the human tragedy and the loss of human life in conflict'. However, he declares it to be 'a lie' that 'the British Government can defeat the IRA'. So he looks forward to 'the end of the day' when 'these problems will be resolved by representatives of the Irish people sitting down with the government and assisting it to leave the country'.[3] Each reader must make up his or her mind as to who will have won in another twenty years' time, as to who is likely to be ruling then in Northern Ireland and South Africa.

These are debatable matters. In such 'internal' wars, the 'justice' claimed for one side or the other may not be so evident to the disinterested observer. This must not distract us from vigorous pursuit of what we believe to be justice and from forceful (if need be) struggle against injustice, so long as there is any reasonable hope of victory. There is no place in Christianity for shoulder-shrugging cynicism and neutralism, for the disinterested and unconcerned spectator. Reinhold Niebuhr wrote in 1969: 'If a season of violence can establish a just social system and can create the possibilities of its preservation, there is no purely ethical ground upon which violence . . . can be ruled out.'[4] Injustice ought to be a goad to drive people into action.

In the midst of the violence of international war, with the British Expeditionary Force in France and Belgium in May 1940, I was surprised and saddened to find young British soldiers who felt that there was nothing to choose between the political systems of Great Britain and Hitlerite Germany. There may well be similar ignorance today, owing to inadequate teaching of history and of civics in many of our schools. It is worth while to review briefly the significance of the anti-Nazi War of 1939, in order to perceive clearly how a war with a reasonable chance of victory can be justified for the Christian.

The Allied Powers went to war in September 1939 basically in order to prevent the spread of an anti-human system which was crushing justice and freedom over more and more of Europe. Hitler was an extraordinary man, a master of mass emotion, whose personality and oratory seemed to cause him to have an almost hypnotic influence over his people. Indeed, thirteen million Germans chose to vote for him. Alan Bullock writes of his 'pursuit of unlimited power; the scorn for justice or any restraint on power; the exaltation of will over reason and conscience; the assertion of an arrogant supremacy; the contempt for others' rights'. He goes on concerning him:

> Cynical and calculating in the exploitation of his histrionic gifts, he retained an unshaken belief in his historic role and in himself as a creature of destiny. . . . The passions which ruled Hitler's mind were ignoble: hatred, resentment, the lust to dominate, to destroy. . . . Even power he conceived of in the crudest terms: an endless vista of military roads, SS garrisons, and concentration camps to sustain the rule of the Aryan 'master race' over the degraded subject peoples of his new empire in the east.

He retained to the end 'an uncanny gift of personal magnetism which defies analysis'.[5] Robert Harris, writing in *The Observer* of 18 September 1988, claims that 'we now know that Hitler was a uniquely wicked man', but adds that in 1938 he did not appear unique.[6] To those of us who were then adult and students of history and politics, he did then appear unique, both in personal evil and in personal demonic influence over a large area of the Western world. A newspaper of 9 November 1938 wrote of the 'night of the long flames' as 'an orgy of violence and arson', of 'a reign of terror without precedent in modern times in a civilized country' for the Jews.

Hitler not only took over Austria and invaded and divided up Czechoslovakia; but he also threatened all Eastern Europe. His Blackshirts and Brownshirts persecuted, mocked, robbed and arrested the Jews of Germany; it seems that it was not until 1942 that he decided to exterminate them. On my desk is a photograph of a tall German soldier about to shoot through her neck a Jewish woman with a child in her arms. Hitler filled German prisons and concentration camps with liberals, socialists and communists. It was known that there were already 65 concentration camps in August 1933. The gentle people whom I visited in Frankfurt in 1936, and most of my liberal-minded

young German friends, quietly disappeared, never, so far as I
know, to be seen again. We foreigners were free to go to
Germany to probe discreetly, to listen, to watch and to keep
quiet or to speak only in whispers where no whisper could be
heard. I listened to Cardinal Faulhaber in the Domkirche in
Munich preaching on the Feast of the Assumption, 15 August
1936. He spoke boldly to an enormous congregation in a big
church: 'Jesus is King and Mary is Queen. Whoever reigns in
Germany, still Jesus is King and Mary is Queen.' The
Brownshirts in the congregation stirred uneasily. I was glad to
get out of Germany and breathe the free air of Austria, still at
that time independent. The old Germany we had known
before 1933 had ceased to be. The hideous strength of Nazi
tyranny had closed in upon the forces of truth and decency
and licensed those of prejudice, hatred and malice. With the
final take-over of Czechoslovakia in March 1939, the British
began to understand what had happened and was happening.
Without a war, it seems that there would have been no
prospect of a revival of freedom and justice in Germany.
Adolf Wagner, Gauleiter of Bavaria, spoke on 4 September
1934 of 'a thousand years of Nazi rule to come'.

It was because of the magnitude of the injustice that Nazism
represented and because of the obvious impossibility of
reform from within that many of us thoughtfully and the
majority of us intuitively went to war in 1939. For myself,
patriotism played no part in my decision to 'join up' in 1939. I
have outlined in some detail, for the benefit of those who
were not then alive and who have not studied that period of
history, the evils which enabled Christians in Britain to
reconcile themselves to taking part in a war in which they
would, tragically, be killing. Dr Peter Hinchliff, whose writing
I greatly admire, tells us concerning killing that 'even where
we recognize that violence is necessary, even when it can be
described as "deserved", there is something dehumanizing
about it'.[7] I do not believe this to be true, despite the

sadnesses, indeed the tragedies, of violence. I have seen with the troops in France and Belgium in 1940, and with the same and other troops in 1944 and 1945 in Burma, young Englishmen killing the enemy at short range. What they did was done without the slightest anger or hatred (except on one occasion when there had been some terrible Japanese cruelty). I neither saw then, nor have I seen since in my contacts with many of the men concerned over the post-war years, any sign of dehumanization. My present Lancashire house-guest, once a pupil of mine, on one occasion killed ninety Japanese with depth-charges dropped on to a submarine from a Catalina flying boat one hundred and fifty miles east of Madras. At the time he felt no more hatred or emotion of any kind than would a window-cleaner or a chimney-sweep at his work. The words are his. He is a wise and gentle man, the father of an outstanding priest. I detect no signs of dehumanization in him.

From a Christian and a humanistic point of view, it was almost impossible in 1939 to refrain from the fight. Although some good pacifists, supporters of the Peace Pledge Union and others, managed to maintain their 'conscientious objection' to the end, many sincere young Christians found themselves quite unable to continue to do nothing in the face of growing and militant evil. One such was a pupil and friend of mine. A few days before he fell 16,000 feet from the air in the course of a Fleet Air Arm practice flight in September 1941, Jim Pomfret wrote to his parents a letter to be opened by them in the event of his death:

I believe in these things for which I have joined in the fight. I believe in them with all my being ... My physical being has been given as a contribution to the defence of the spiritual things in which I believe, the things which I know in my heart are what really matter ... I have come to realize the completely overriding importance of the things of the spirit; nothing is too costly to put before their preservation.

He was not particularly religious, but was thinking of the
freedom of the human mind. The letter is dated 14 September
1941 and was written from Yeovilton, Somerset. He was killed
on 19 September. I saw a host of letters to his parents, mostly
from men a little older than himself, testifying to his sheer
goodness and to his influence for good on his contemporaries.

It was for the defence of 'spiritual things', of freedom and
justice, that an essentially gentle but wise and thoughtful lad
of twenty-three was prepared not only to die but to kill. It is a
very serious thing for a Christian and humanist to make up his
mind to be prepared to take life. Fifty million lives were lost
in the Second World War. It was a terrible price to pay for the
restoration of justice and freedom over an enormous area of
Europe and for the prevention of the spread of Nazi tyranny
to most of it. If the war had not been fought hundreds of
millions of Europeans would have been deprived of justice
and freedom, of the right to think freely, read freely, speak
freely, perhaps for generations . The consequence of not acting
forcefully against incarnate evil would have been far worse in
its totality for humanity than the fighting of a war. Justice and
freedom for human beings somehow have to be defended.
'We do not just have to count heads, to decide on the "greater
evil". We have to try to assess the cost in terms of human
repression, exploitation and victimization.'[8] When we consider
the rightness (or wrongness) of other 'wars', of the Soviet
armed interference in Afghanistan and of the US invasion of
Grenada in 1983 and the attack upon Libya in April 1986, we
have to ask ourselves if such taking and risking of life was as
justified from a Christian and humane viewpoint as was the
War of September 1939. I find it impossible to believe that
United States support for Nicaraguan 'Contras' can possibly
be defended in the sense in which I have defended a war
genuinely fought for justice and freedom between 1939 and
1945.

In the Union Society debate at Oxford on 5 March 1987 in

which Gerry Adams took part, the abhorrence of educated modern youth for that violence which kills was demonstrated in speech after speech. 'All sane human beings ...', said one speaker, 'detest violence and will choose any course that has a chance of holding it off.' Gerry Adams, who made a most moderate and conciliatory speech, was voted down by an enormous majority. Let educated youth, detesting violence, use its eloquence and vehemence in attacking governments which commit acts of war in cases where there is no outraged justice and interminable injustice to require the military rescue of a people. Let them, if need be, give of their enthusiasm and idealism in the cause of rescuing the weak at the risk, if need be, of their own lives. Let us all learn that war is only needed in the occasional desperate case where injustice seems to be unending and incapable of yielding to anything except to war. Hannah Arendt writes that 'violence, being instrumental by nature, is rational to the extent that it is effective in reaching the end that must justify it'.[9] She goes on to quote William O'Brien, a nineteenth-century agrarian and nationalist agitator, who said that sometimes violence is the only way of ensuring a hearing for moderation. This small book is intended to demonstrate this.

The Lambeth Conference of 1988 chose to express 'understanding' for 'those who, after exhausting all other ways, choose the way of armed struggle'. It chose, a few days later, to exempt Northern Ireland from this understanding. However, the point has been made. Thomas Merton wrote that 'the theology of love must seek to deal realistically with the evil and injustice in the world and not merely to compromise with them'. 'The non-violent ideal', he added, 'does not contain in itself all the answers to all our questions.' There are injustices and there is lack of freedom in the Soviet Union, we believe. There is nothing we can do about that in a military sense. Mercifully we begin to see the development in the USSR of a 'glasnost', of a new 'openness', with hope for a more free and just society there. Elsewhere, as we have seen, there are powers less mighty than that of Russia. Their suffering peoples ought not to be made to wait so long as the Russians have waited for a 'glasnost'. Here and there revolution to remedy injustice is practicable and sometimes needs to be supported. Intermittent violence over a long period may well need to be used in the hope of avoiding full-scale revolution. In cases of revolution and of war, fine young lives may have to be lost, and the innocent killed; but also there is resurrection.

CHAPTER SEVEN

What Now?

This short essay has been written to defend the use of force, and if need be of violence, where there is enduring injustice and where there seems to be a reasonable chance of successfully replacing it with a just order. It is written to provoke thought and to challenge those who are prepared to do nothing or next to nothing in the face of injustice to others. It is intended to impress Christians and others with the enormous importance for human beings of justice. It is my hope that it may lead to individual study and to group discussions concerning the whole Christian and philosophical concept of justice. I believe that the doctrine of justice requires study as a whole. It is simply not good enough to take a few verses from the Sermon on the Mount (or elsewhere) and say that they define our duty. God has been revealing his will for us in scripture and through the Spirit and we have to work hard to get the message. We learn slowly. By the end of the eighteenth century we had even learnt that slavery was wrong. The lesson had taken a long time in the learning. I am anxious for Christians and others to start anew in their study of the doctrine of justice. It is a doctrine which requires careful study. I believe such study will be rewarding for human beings and for the practice of love. Some Christian doctrines seem today to be of comparatively little significance. The doctrine of the (Immaculate) Conception of the Blessed Virgin Mary is not in our day a burning issue. The Christian doctrine of justice has immediate significance for the starving people of Ethiopia and the Sudan, for the storm-and-flood-ravaged people of Bangladesh, for the suffering Palestinians, for the under-privileged of South Africa. Or at least it would have great significance if people took it seriously. A serious study of justice will lead those who follow it to look hard at the conditions under which injustice for human beings reigns. It will surely challenge them to consider what can be done about it. We Christians all know that it is our duty to love our neighbours. The study of justice will teach us all that the foundation needed to fulfil the duty of love of others is the making sure, to the utmost of our ability, that they secure justice.

Years ago, after I had spoken to a women's meeting about justice, the parish priest remarked to me that he had never thought of justice in connection with religion. My heart sank, as I realized anew the measure of the ignorance of many Christians about one of the traditional 'cardinal virtues'. This ignorance and lack of serious thought concerning justice is illustrated again by the apparent satisfaction with which most of the members of the two great political parties and the electors of Britain as a whole regard our unjust electoral system. Not only a minority of those eligible to vote, but a minority of those who did vote in 1987, elected a large majority of Members of Parliament pledged to policies contrary to the wishes of the majority of the voters. In 1987, on 11 June, 57.8% of those who voted did so for parties other than the Conservative Party. 55.2% of those who voted did so for Labour or for the Alliance or for the Scottish and Welsh

Nationalist Parties. 53.5% were for Labour and the Alliance. It is obviously unjust that the Conservative Party should be empowered to act as if it commanded a clear majority of the voters. It commands a minority. A people who cared about justice at home and abroad would not tolerate a system which patently works unjustly when other and more just electoral systems are available. I only use this to illustrate our need for education in a great and vital philosophical and religious principle. I should like to think that this small book might challenge some to thought and some to the kind of self-and-mutual education so many of us need.

The man in the street does know what justice means, education or no education. When your profits are going up and his wages are staying down, he will very rightly accuse you of 'injustice'. If he wants to pay you a huge compliment, he will say of you to his mate: 'I don't like the way he talks, but I will say that he's a just man.' What we Christians and others need to do is to encourage as many as possible to think more frequently of justice for others, at home and abroad, as well as for themselves. Long ago, F. P. Harton wrote in his *Elements of the Spiritual Life* rather beautifully concerning justice: 'Justice is the glad and constant rendering to others of their rights.'[1] Christians, I am sure, all human beings, I think, ought to be challenged, ought to challenge themselves, whenever they read or otherwise hear of injustice. The question ought to be: 'What are we going to do about it?' It is a terrible thing to stand by and do nothing. Love begins when we make up our minds that if it is possible justice must be done, when we agree that we will do our utmost to force justice to be done.

Notes

Chapter One   Force and the Gospel

1. Dennis Nineham, *The Use and Abuse of the Bible*, reissued SPCK 1978, pp. 111, 102, 146.
2. Quoted by R. Harries, *Should a Christian support Guerillas?*, Lutterworth Press 1982, p. 4.
3. Karl Rahner, *Theological Investigations*, Vol. 4, Darton, Longman and Todd 1966, p. 399.
4. *City of God*, IV, 4.
5. Quoted in J. G. Davies, *Christians, Politics and Violent Revolution*, SCM Press 1976, p. 41.
6. Bruce Chilton and J. I. H. McDonald, *Jesus and the Ethics of the Kingdom*, SPCK 1987, p. 6.
7. J. L. Houlden, *Ethics and the New Testament*, reissued Mowbrays 1975, pp. 7–8.
8. Paul Tillich, *Political Expectations*, Harper & Row, NY 1971, pp. 120f.

Chapter Two   Justice

1. R. Harries, op. cit., p. 13.
2. P. Tillich, op. cit., p. 120.
3. Bruno Snell, *The Discovery of the Mind*, Harper & Row, NY 1960, pp. 249–50.
4. Plato, *The Republic*, IV, 434.
5. *The Ethics of Aristotle*, trans. J. A. K. Thomson, Penguin 1976, 51134B.
6. Ernest Barker, *Political Thought of Plato and Aristotle*, Dover Publications 1959, p. 241.
7. N. H. Snaith, *Distinctive Ideas of the Old Testament*, Epworth Press 1974, p. 74.
8. Thomas Aquinas, *Summa Theologica*, 11, 2Q58, A1.
9. Ibid., 11, 2Q58, A5.
10. Ibid., 11, 2Q58, A12.
11. A.J. Carlyle, 'The Mediaeval Theory of Social Order in Charles Gore (ed.), *Return of Christendom*, Allen & Unwin 1922, p. 177.

12. Emil Brunner, *Justice and the Social Order*, Lutterworth Press 1949, pp. 117–118.

13. John Bennett, 'Love and Justice' in R. H. Preston (ed.), *Theology and Change*, SCM Press 1975, pp. 138, 142.

14. 15 January 1988, p. 12.

15. See K. D. Kaunda, *Kaunda on Violence*, Collins 1980.

Chapter Three   Three Men of Peace

1. R. K. Prabhu and U. R. Rao, *The Mind of Mahatma Gandhi*, OUP 1945, p. 66.

2. J. Simkin, *Gandhi*, Spartacus 1987, p. 23.

3. V. Mehta, *Mahatma Gandhi and His Apostles*, Penguin 1977, p. 14–15.

4. J. Simkin, op. cit., pp. 24–5.

5. V. Mehta, op. cit., p. 132.

6. M. K. Gandhi, *An Autobiography* or *The Story of my Experiments with Truth*, 1927; reissued Penguin 1982, p. 163.

7. V. Mehta, op. cit., p. 146.

8. Ibid., p. 148.

9. Ibid., p. 153.

10. From the Marquess of Hastings' private journal entry for 17 May 1918, quoted by P. M. Bazaz in *Indo-British Review*, April–September 1971, p. 22.

11. H. V. Hodson, *The Great Divide*, Hutchinson 1969, p. 106.

12. See. R. Gopal, *How India Struggled for Freedom*, Book Centre, Bombay 1967, pp. 430–1, and other similar books.

13. F. G. Hutchins, *Spontaneous Revolution*, Manohar Book Service 1971, p. 278.

14. M. Gupta, *History of the Indian Revolutionary Movement*, Samaya Publications, Bombay 1972, p. 227.

15. H. V. Hodson, op. cit., p. 106.

16. Quoted by M. Gupta, op. cit., p. 253.

17. See R. J. Moore, *Escape from Empire*, Clarendon Press 1983, p. 1.

18. Ibid., p. 10.

19. S. B. Oates, *Let the Trumpet Sound*, New American Library 1982, p. 31.

20. See A. M. Schlesinger, *Robert Kennedy and his Times*, André Deutsch 1978, p. 337.

21. See D. J. Garrow, *Bearing the Cross*, Random House, NY 1988, p. 24.

22. Ibid., p. 58.

23. Ibid., p. 68.

24. Ibid., p. 81.

NOTES

25. Ibid., p. 72.
26. See A. M. Schlesinger, op. cit., p. 215.
27. D. J. Garrow, op. cit., p. 282.
28. Ibid., p. 284.
29. Ibid., pp. 313, 375, 617 et passim.
30. A. M. Schlesinger, op. cit., pp. 362–3.
31. *D. J. Garrow, op. cit., pp. 602, 611, 614 et passim.*
32. Sermon, 13 April 1967, in King Papers, King Center, Atlanta.
33. Quoted by E. Bethge, *Dietrich Bonhoeffer*, Collins 1970, p. 331.
34. E. H. Robertson, *The Shame and the Sacrifice*, Hodder and Stoughton 1987, p. 20.
35. During his 1974 Mackintosh Lecture.
36. E. Bethge, op. cit., p. 697.
37. Ibid., p. 536.
38. Dietrich Bonhoeffer, *Letters and Papers from Prison*, Enlarged Edition, SCM Press 1971, pp. 16–17.
39. E. Bethge, op. cit., p. 659.
40. Dietrich Bonhoeffer, *Ethics*, SCM Press 1955, p. 214.
41. E. Bethge, op. cit., p. 682.
42. Ibid., p. 727.
43. Ibid., p. 831.

Chapter Four   Violence in Northern Ireland

1. Sean MacBride, in his Introduction to B. Sands, *One Day in My Life*, Pluto Press 1983, pp. 9, 20.
2. J. G. Simms, *War and Politics in Ireland 1649–1730*, Hambledon Press 1986, p. 65.
3. Quoted by B. Sands, op. cit., p. 20.
4. D. E. Apter, *Rethinking Development*, Sage Publications 1987, p. 254.
5. N. Mansergh, *The Irish Question 1840–1923*, George Allen & Unwin, 3rd edition 1975, pp. 73, 146.
6. Lawlor, *Britain and Ireland 1914–23*, Gill & Macmillan 1983, p. 41.
7. C. Woodham-Smith, *The Great Hunger*, Hamish Hamilton 1962, pp. 441, 407, 368, 412.
8. N. Mansergh, *The Irish Question 1840–1926*, George Allen & Unwin 1975, p. 74.
9. J. M. Curran, *Birth of the Irish Free State*, University of Alabama Press 1980, p. 13.
10. *A Report on Religious and Political Discrimination*, HMSO 1987, p. 24.
11. Ibid., p. 35.
12. *The Guardian*, 30 December, 1987, p. 4.

13. *A Report on Religious and Political Discrimination*, p. 40.
14. Ibid., p. 42.
15. Des Wilson, *An End to Silence*, Royal Carbery Books, Cork 1985, 1987 edition, p. 62.
16. Ibid., p. 67.
17. Ibid., p. 7.
18. Denis Faul and Raymond Murphy, *British Army and Special Branch RUC Brutalities*, Abbey Printers, Cavan 1974.
19. B. Sands, op. cit.
20. Produced by a 'Concerned Relatives and Ex-Prisoners Committee'.
21. P. Bishop & E. Mallie, *The Provisional IRA*, Heinemann 1987, p. 246.
22. Ibid., p. 203.
23. Ibid., p. 159.
24. *Sunday Times*, Irish edition, 10 July 1988, p. 1.
25. *The Guardian*, 25 November 1988, p. 24.
26. R. Harries, op. cit., p. 43.
27. P. Bishop & E. Mallie, op. cit., p. 141.
28. In D. Beresford, *Ten Men Dead*, Grafton Books 1987, p. 359.
29. Ibid., p. 388.
30. P. Bishop & E. Mallie, op. cit., pp. 213–14.
31. Des Wilson, op. cit., p. 49.
32. Quoted by B. Sands, op. cit., p. 21.
33. Des Wilson, op. cit., p. 52.
34. *The Guardian*, 3 December 1988.
35. *The Times*, 3 May 1988, p. 16.
36. P. 1.
37. *The Observer*, 29 January 1989, p. 2.
38. *The Independent*, 30 January 1989, p. 6.
39. *The Daily Telegraph*, 1 February 1989, p. 1.

Chapter Five   Palestine, South Africa, Central and South America

1. Colin Chapman, *Whose Promised Lane?*, 2nd revd edn, Lion 1985, p. 19.
2. *The Guardian*, 2 August 1988, p. 18.
3. Quoted by Colin Chapman, op. cit., p. 49.
4. *The Observer*, 14 February 1988, p. 10.
5. 1988 *Report* of the West Bank Project.
6. *The Observer*, 31 July 1988, p. 21.
7. G. Rowley, *Israel into Palestine*, Mansell 1984, p. 57.
8. CAABU, 1 June 1987.
9. Report by Amnesty International, *Israel and the Occupied Territories*, June 1988.

10. *The Observer*, 31 July 1988, p. 21.
11. Al-Haq, *20 Years of Israeli Occupation* (Briefing Paper 1).
12. *The Observer*, 14 February 1988, p. 10.
13. *The Observer*, 7 August 1988, p. 21.
14. Ibid., p. 23.
15. A. Keppell-Jones, *South Africa*, 5th revd edn, Hutchinson 1975, p. 177.
16. Quoted by T. R. H. Davenport, *South Africa*, 2nd edn, Macmillan 1987, p. 270.
17. Quoted by A. Gallicinos and J. Rogers, *Southern Africa*, Pluto, London 1978, p. 52.
18. Davenport, op. cit., p. 271.
19. *The Observer*, 12 June 1988, p. 21.
20. *Wall Street Journal*, 22 April 1988, p. 1.
21. Steve Biko, *I Write What I Like*, Penguin 1988, p. 88.
22. *The Tablet*, 16 July 1988, p. 806.
23. Leonard Sweetman in his Foreword to A. Boesak, *Black and Reformed*, Shotaville, Johannesburg 1984, p. xi.
24. K. D. Kaunda, *Kaunda on Violence*, Collins 1980, p. 11.
25. Ibid., p. 28.
26. Ibid., p. 58.
27. Ibid., pp. 168, 170.
28. Ibid., pp. 174, 178.
29. Ibid., p. 97.
30. A. Boesak, op. cit., pp. 88, 87.
31. *The Tablet*, 16 July 1988, p. 804.
32. Jean-Marc Ela, *From Charity to Liberation*, Catholic Institute for International Relations 1984, p. 19.
33. A. Rooper, *Fragile Victory*, Weidenfeld & Nicolson 1987, p. 41.
34. *The Guardian*, 28 November 1988, p. 23.
35. P. Erdozaín, *Archbishop Romero*, Lutterworth Press 1981, p. 27.
36. D. H. Levine (ed.), *Religion and Political Conflict in Latin America*, University of North Carolina Press 1986, p. 59.
37. Peter Hinchliff, *Holiness and Politics*, Darton, Longman and Todd 1982, pp. 195, 197, 196.
38. Christopher Rowland, *Radical Christianity*, Polity Press 1988, pp. 9, 116, 127, 131.
39. In G. Gutierrez, *A Theology of Liberation*, revd edn, SCM Press 1988. Gutierrez is quoting an untranslated article by W. Pannenberg.
40. Ibid., pp. 152, 157.
41. Ibid., pp. 165, 164.
42. I am grateful to the Reverend Peter West, of Church Action for Central America, for information quoted here.
43. P. Erdozaín, op. cit., p. 75.

44. Ibid., p. 80.
45. P. Freire, *Pedagogy of the Oppressed*, Penguin 1985, pp. 41, 43.
46. D. H. Levine and A. W. Wilde, 'The Catholic Church, Politics and Violence', in the *Review of Politics*, vol. 39, no. 2, pp. 200–49.
47. Ibid., p. 245.
48. Ibid., p. 232.
49. P. Freire, op. cit., p. 131.
50. Segundo Galilea, 'Liberation Theology and New Tasks Facing Christians' in R. Gibellini (ed.), *Frontiers and Theology in Latin America*, SCM Press 1980, p. 166.
51. P. Walker, *Rediscovering the Middle Way*, Mowbray 1988, p. 96.
52. Phillip Berryman, *Religious Roots of Rebellion*, SCM Press 1984, pp. 316, 317.
53. Louie G. Hechanova, *The Gospel and Struggle*, Catholic Institute for International Relations 1986, p. 22.

Chapter Six   War

1. *The Guardian*, 26 May 1987, p. 12.
2. Keith Ward, 'The Just War and Nuclear Arms' in F. Bridger (ed.), *The Cross and the Bomb*, Mowbray 1983, p. 47.
3. *The Guardian*, 25 August 1988, p. 17.
4. Reinhold Niebuhr, *Moral Man and Immoral Society*, SCM Press 1963, p. 179.
5. A. Bullock, *Hitler – A Study in Tyranny*, revd edn, Odhams 1964, pp. 805, 804.
6. P. 13.
7. Peter Hinchliff, op. cit., p. 62.
8. Keith Ward, art. cit., p. 55.
9. H. Arendt, *On Violence*, Allen Lane, Penguin Press 1970, p. 79.

Chapter Seven   What Now?

1. F. P. Harton, *Elements of the Spiritual Life*, SPCK 1932, p. 64.

Index

Adams, Gerry, 38, 46, 49, 52, 92, 98
Advisory Commission on Human
  Rights, 45
Afghanistan, 97
African National Congress, 71, 72,
  73, 74, 92
Ali Awwad al-Jammal, 58
Ambrose, St, 92
America, South and Central, 14, 32,
  37, 80–88
  see also Argentina, Brazil, Chile,
  Colombia, El Salvador,
  Guatemala, Nicaragua
Amnesty International, 58, 64, 71,
  81
Anglo-Irish Agreement, 45
Apter, David, 36, 37
Aquinas, St Thomas, 10, 11, 92
Arab-British Centre, 57
Arendt, Hannah, 98
Argentina, 91
Aristotle, 10, 11
Arlow, Canon Bill, 50
Ascherson, Neal, 75
Attlee, Clement, 22
Augustine, St, 5, 92
Australia, 19
Austria, 94, 95

Baker, John Austin, 36
Balfour Declaration, 54
Bangladesh, 101
Barker, Ernest, 10
Barmen Declaration, 29
Barth, Karl, 28
Base Communities, 80–86

Belafonte, Harry, 27
Belgium, 93, 96
Bell, George, 28, 32
Ben-Gurion, David, 54
Bennett, John, 12
Berryman, Phillip, 87
Bethge, Eberhard, 29, 31
Biko, Steve, 69, 73f.
Boesak, Allan, 76, 78
Bonhoeffer, Dietrich, 6, 14, 28–33
Boyne, Battle of the, 36
Brazil, 84, 85
Brunner, Emil, 12
Buchenwald, 32
Bullock, Alan, 93f.
Bultmann, Rudolf, 6
Burke, Edmund, 10

Carlyle, A. J., 12
Cassidy, Sheila, 81
Ceannt, Eamonn, 40
Central America see America, South
  and Central
Chamberlain, Neville, xi, 14
Chikane, Frank, 75, 79
Chile, 81, 85, 86
Chilton, Bruce, 6
Clarke, Thomas J., 40
Colombia, 81, 86, 87
Commission of the Churches on
  International Affairs, 58
Commission on Human Rights, 45
Commonwealth Eminent Persons
  Group, 74
Comunidades de base see Base
  Communities

Connolly, James, 40
'Contras', 80, 97
Cripps, Stafford, 18
Cuba, 80
Czechoslovakia, xi, 91, 94, 95

Dahriyyeh, 60f.
Dakar Declaration, 74
Daladier, Edouard, xi
Declaration Act of 1689, 36
Dohnanyi, Hans, 30, 32
Dunkirk, 4
Durham Report, 22

Easter Rising, 40
Eban, Abba, 55, 67
Ela, Jean-Marc, 79
El Salvador, 81, 82, 85, 86, 87
Enniskillen, 44, 48, 49, 52
Ethiopia, 101
European Economic Community, 64

Falkland Islands, 91
Faul, Denis, 47
Faulhaber, Cardinal, 95
Fellowship of Reconciliation, 23
Fitt, Gerry, 45
France, 14, 93, 96
Freiburg Memorandum, 32
Freire, Paulo, 86

Gandhi, M. K., 13, 15, 16–22, 23,
    24, 28, 77
Garrow, David, 25, 26
Gaza Strip, 8, 13, 37, 55, 56, 57, 65
Germany, ix, x, 14, 18, 27, 29, 30,
    37, 42, 44, 55, 66, 90, 93, 94, 95
Gilmour, Ian, 56, 65
Gladstone, William Ewart, 38
Golan Heights, 55
Grenada, 92, 97
Guatemala, 87
Gutierrez, G., 84

Harnack, Adolf, 28
Harries, Richard, Bishop of Oxford,
    3, 49
Harris, Robert, 94

Hartley, Tom, 46, 47, 48
Harton, F. P., 102
Hastings, Marquess of, 19
Hattersley, Roy, 40, 51
Haughey, Charles, 51
Hechanova, Louie G., CSSR, 32, 88
Hellwig, M. K., 87
Herzl, Theodor, 53
Hinchliff, Peter, 83, 95
Hitler, Adolf, ix, xi, 14, 27, 28, 29,
    30, 31, 93, 94
Hoare, Samuel, 14
Hodson, H. V., 19, 21
Houlden, J. L., 6
Humphrey, Hubert, 27
Hungary, 29

India, 16, 18, 19, 20, 21
Indian National Congress, 17, 20
Institute for Contextual Theology,
    83
International Commission of Jurists,
    60
Iran, 90
Iraq, 90
Ireland, 12, 34–52, 93, 98
Irish Council of Churches, 50
Irish Republican Army (IRA), 34,
    35, 48, 49, 50, 92
Irwin, Lord, 18
Israel, 12, 13, 37, 53–58
    see also Gaza Strip, Occupied
    Territories, West Bank
Israeli Defence Force, 65
Italy, 37, 42, 44

Japan, 18, 37
Jaspers, Karl, 5
Jerrold, Douglas, 77
Jews, x, 29, 53, 54, 55, 68, 94
Johnson, Lyndon, 26, 27
Johnson, Paul, 51

Kairos Document, 76
Kaufman, Gerald, 13
Kaunda, Kenneth, 14, 15, 77f.
Kennedy, Jacqueline, 27
Kennedy, John, 25, 26

Kennedy, Robert, 25, 27
King, Martin Luther, 13, 15, 22–27

Lambeth Conference, 9, 12, 77, 79, 98
Laski, Harold, x
Latin America, see America, South and Central
League of Nations, 54
Liberation theology, 80–88
Libya, 97
Linlithgow, Lord, 20
Lloyd George, David, 38
Long Kesh Prison, 50
Lusaka Document, 76

MacBride, Sean, 35
MacDiarmada, Sean, 40
McDonagh, Thomas, 40
McDonald, J. I. H., 6
McElwee, Tom, 50
McFarlane, Brendan, 50
McGuinness, Martin, 52
Macaulay, Thomas Babington, 19
Magilligan Prison, 47
Mandela, Nelson, 72f., 74
Marais, Etienne, 68
Medellín, 14, 81, 82, 83, 85, 87
Mehta, V., 18
Merton, Thomas, 98
Montagu-Chelmsford Report, 19
Morrison, Danny, 50
Mountbatten, Lord, 22
Munich, xi, 14
Munro, Thomas, 19
Murphy, Raymond, 47
Mussolini, B., xi

NATO, 89, 90, 91
Nehru, Jawaharlal, 16, 20, 22
Nicaragua, 80, 81, 85, 87, 97
Niebuhr, Reinhold, 93
Nineham, Dennis, 2f.
Nixon, Richard, 27
Northern Ireland, see Ireland

O'Brien, Conor Cruise, 52
O'Brien, William, 98

Occupied Territories, 55–67
Osborne, Sydney Godolphin, 39

Pakistan, 20
Palestine see Israel; also Gaza Strip, Occupied Territories, West Bank
Palestine Liberation Organization (PLO), 64, 66
Peace Pledge Union, 96
Pearse, P. H., 40
Pinochet, General, 81
Pius XII, Pope, 9, 12
Plato, 10
Plunket, Joseph, 40
Pomfret, Jim, 96f.

Rahner, Karl, 3
Reagan, Ronald, 90
Reid, Joe, 46, 48
Republic of Ireland, see Ireland
Rivonia case, 72
Romero, Oscar, 81f., 86
Round Table Conference, 20
Rowland, Christopher, 80, 83
Royal Ulster Constabulary (RUC), 41f., 47
Rupp, Gordon, 29
Rustin, Bayard, 24

Sandinista Government, 80
Sands, Bobby, 47, 50
September, Reginald, 73
Shamir, Yizhak, 13, 67
Shaull, Roger, 83
Sinden, Gabriel, SSM, 65
Sinn Fein, 34, 35, 44, 46, 47, 48, 52
Smiley, Richard, 24
Smith, Ian, 77
Snaith, N. H., 11
Snell, Bruno, 10
Somoza family, 80, 81
South Africa, 8, 12, 14, 17, 20, 68–79, 93, 101
South African Council of Churches, 75
South America, see America, Central and South

Southern Negro Leaders Conference (SNLC), 24, 25
Soviet Union, 14, 55, 90, 91, 97, 98, 99
Springhill Community, 42f.
Stubbs, Aelred, CR, 73
Suarez, Francisco de, 10
Sudan, 101

Tabor, Robert, 49
Tawney, R. H., x
Taylor, John V., 68
Tillich, Paul, 7, 10
Torres, Camilo, 87
Tutu, Desmond, 78, 79

Ulster Defence Regiment (UDR), 42, 49
United Nations, 55, 64, 66

United States, 14, 67, 80, 90, 91, 92, 97

Verwoerd, H., 69

Wagner, Adolf, 13, 95
Wallace, George, 23, 26
West, Peter, 80
West Bank, 8, 54, 55, 56, 57, 58, 66, 68
Wilson, Des, 42, 45, 46, 51
Woodham-Smith, Cecil, 39
Woodward, C. Vann, 26
World Alliance of Reformed Churches, 76

Yeats, W. B., 50

Zangwill, Israel, 53
Zionism, 53